Selected Sketches of Dodge County, Georgia History

Selected Sketches of Dodge County, Georgia History

Edited by Stephen Whigham for the Society

Presented by the Dodge Historical Society
2019

©Copyright 2019 Dodge Historical Society
P.O. Box 163, Eastman, Georgia 31023

©Copyright administered by MMJW BookHouse, LLC
P. O. Box 111, Eastman, Georgia 31023

Published by MMJW BookHouse by arrangement with the Dodge Historical Society

For additional information: http://www.lightwood.com

All rights reserved. Copyright under Berne Copyright Convention, and Pan-American Copyright Convention. No part of this book may be reproduced, stored in a retrieval system, or transmitted in any form, or by any means, electronic, mechanical, photocopying, recording, or otherwise, without prior permission of the author.

ISBN: 978-0-9864060-3-4 (Trade Paperback)
First Edition

Contents

Preface: A Guide to the Reader

1.	Early Citizens	1
2.	Homes, Hotels and Other Buildings	55
3.	Towns and Communities of Dodge County	83
4.	Illustrations	113
5.	Remembrances of Days Gone By	133
6.	Culture, Leisure, The Arts and Community Life	157
7.	Formation of the Dodge Historical Society	179
8.	The Dodge Historical Society Cemetery Project	185

Acknowledgements 195
Suggested Readings 199
Index 206

Preface
A Guide for the Reader

In books lies the soul of the whole Past Time; the articulate audible voice of the Past, when the body and material substance of it has altogether vanished like a dream.
—*Thomas Carlyle (1795-1881), Historian*

The material presented to the reader in the following pages derives primarily from newsletters distributed by the Dodge Historical Society. Beginning around 1994, the newsletters were mailed to Society members announcing upcoming meeting dates. This was in the early days before the Internet and email had become widespread. The mailing consisted of a cover page with the meeting details and also included a half-page application form for prospective members.

Early on, the mailings began including a short historical piece, at first written mostly by Martha Saunders or Chester Saunders. These features usually ran to no more than a single-spaced typed page. As an early member of the Society, I received these "mailers" and the first thing I did was to read the historical material. Topics such as various houses in early Eastman, local hotels, special events and other writings provided a glimpse into the history of Dodge County people and places. Later items were written by Tad Evans, Irene Gregory, Olin Pound, Ovid Vickers and John D. Willcox and unidentified others. The works add up to a valuable set of historical vignettes covering a wide range of topics.

This book originates with Mary Johnson Jowers. Ms. Jowers grew up in Eastman. She retained a large number of the original newsletters. Members of the Historical Society asked that a book be produced consisting of the newsletter material.

As editor, I used all of the newsletter material and added the biographical study on William Pitt Eastman prepared by Tad Evans and John D. Willcox for the *History of Dodge County, 1932-1992*.

The reader will note that some of the items end with a date and occasionally with a name. The name is the author of the particular piece. Not all items designated an author or a date. Further, this collection is by no means a complete history of Dodge County's rich heritage. It is a selection derived from the available newsletters.

For those interested in deeper study of Dodge's history, a list of suggested readings is presented at the end of this work. A good starting point is the *History of Dodge County* by Mrs. Wilton P. Cobb, published in 1932. Next, the excellent follow-up to that book is the *History of Dodge County, 1932-1992*, compiled by members of the Dodge Historical Society and published in 1993. Both studies are rewarding reading for those interested.

The contents of this book are divided by general categories into sections based on subject matter. This material is not arranged chronologically. Photographs (Illustrations) augment the historical text. A general Index is included as well and readers are encouraged to consult it for names and places of interest.

A great many of the original founders of the Dodge Historical Society are no longer with us. As the years pass, many of those with direct connection to past times and history in Dodge County are gone. Preserving as much of the record by documenting, preserving, compiling and publishing this historical material is a task to be valued by us all. A final section of the book contains a history of the Historical Society itself and acknowledges the hard work the original founders contributed in the beginning of the organization.

Let us hope our efforts to commit these memories to the page will live on for future generations to savor and enjoy.

Stephen Whigham
Eastman, Georgia
November 2019

EARLY CITIZENS OF DODGE COUNTY

WILLIAM PITT EASTMAN
FOUNDER OF EASTMAN GEORGIA

By Tad Evans and John D. Willcox

The subject of this sketch, the Honorable William Pitt Eastman, was a gentleman of the old school; honest, kindly, well-educated and generous. He was born in Gilmanton, New Hampshire, the son of Ebenezer and Deborah Greeley Eastman, on May 16, 1813, the third son and fourth born of five children. The Eastmans were an old New England family, having descended from Roger Eastman. Roger was born in Wales in 1611, and removed to the Massachusetts Bay Colony in April 1638 on the ship *Confidence*. He settled in Salisbury, Massachusetts. His ninth child and eighth son, Samuel Eastman (1657-1725), married Elizabeth Severance and removed to Kingston, New Hampshire. They had twelve children and died in Kingston. Their fifth child and oldest son, also named Samuel, was born January 5, 1695. He was married in 1728 to Mrs. Sarah (Brown) Clough, with whom he had seven children. He died in Kingston on December 20, 1753. Their sixth child and fourth son, Ebenezer Eastman, was born April 24, 1746 in Kingston. As a Lieutenant in the War for American Independence, he was a Company Commander (in the absence of his Captain) at the Battle of Bunker Hill that occurred on June 17, 1775. His wife, Mary Butler Eastman, whom he had married on November 15, 1773, on the Sunday following the battle while at church, heard about the cannonading coming from the direction of Boston. Alarmed about the safety of her husband, she departed on horseback for the scene of action. There being no real roads, she was guided by blazes on the trees. She carried her babe, Abigail Eastman, about half way, where she left the child with friends and continued on her journey. She arrived at Charlestown and found her husband safe and sound. This incident of the Revolution is described as *Mary Butler's Ride*, the poem by Benjamin F. Taylor. After the Revolution, Lt. Ebenezer Eastman settled in Gilmanton and was a farmer. He and Mary had eleven children, of which Ebenezer, born January 12, 1777 in Gilmanton, and died there on October 9, 1864, was William Pitt Eastman's father.

William Pitt Eastman grew up in Gilmanton and was educated at the famous old Gilmanton Academy, and was for years afterward, one of its trustees. After completing his education, William became a merchant in Gilmanton, buying out Moses P. Page. After about two years he joined his brother Arthur in an enterprise that took them to the western part of Arkansas and Missouri. After being left high and dry for several weeks up the Arkansas River due to low water, they built a flat boat with their own hands and reached safety. After returning home, they formed a partnership in Boston in the grocery and fruit business, where they "made and lost large sums of money." Their partnership lasted eight years. After a time in Boston, he removed to Newark, New Jersey, where he was involved in the manufacture of men and women's woolen underwear. His factory was the largest building in Newark at that time, and his company was capitalized at $200,000, a huge amount in the dollars of that long ago day. He apparently made his fortune during the period in Newark.

Mr. Eastman visited the pine forests of Georgia in 1862 and immediately realized the potential value of this vast area of trees, although at that time, due to inaccessibility, the property was practically worthless. The Macon and Brunswick Railroad had been organized, however, and after the end of the civil war in 1865, construction began to complete the railroad from Macon to Brunswick. The road would run directly through the middle of the pine forest. After spending considerable time in examining the property titles, Mr. Eastman purchased the entire tract of 300,000 acres of prime yellow pine forest that had been owned for many years by a group of gentlemen residing in New York, Boston, Philadelphia, and Baltimore. About 1868, together with A. G. P. Dodge, William Chauncey and others, he formed the Georgia Land and Lumber Company. The President of this company was William E. Dodge, the father of A. G. P., George E., and Norman W. Dodge, and the person for whom Dodge County would be named. The company was capitalized at half a million dollars and owned 400,000 acres of the Georgia land. After a few years, Eastman sold his share in the company, and although he was sometimes their agent in real estate dealings, he no longer had any say-so in the operation of the organization. He retained about 50,000 acres of the Georgia lands for himself.

Early in 1869, William Pitt Eastman, with his wife, the former Helena Dekay Fondey, daughter of Isaac Fondey of Albany, New York, and their daughter, Caro, removed to Georgia. He perhaps made this move hoping to improve his health as he did not appear to be a robust man or it may have been to look for new horizons and to take advantage of the depressed business conditions following the Civil War. In any event, the Eastman family settled in a pine forest at a railroad station on the Macon and

Brunswick Railroad known as Station No. 13. This place at that time amounted to no more than the railroad station, a sawmill, a post office and a few houses. They moved into a small cottage of three rooms located on the property now owned by the Grady Coffee family at Oak Street and 8th Avenue. The original owner of the 405 acres was William (Billy) Lee, an original settler in the area.

While on a trip to Europe with his family, Mr. Eastman received in London a letter from George H. Hazlehurst, President of the Macon and Brunswick Railroad, stating that he had taken the liberty of naming Station No. 13 "Eastman" in honor of Mr. Eastman. Mr. Eastman, knowing that this would somehow cost him money, thanked Mr. Hazlehurst for the complement, but declined the offer. However, upon returning to Station No. 13 five months later, Mr. Eastman found his name on the train depot and printed on the train tickets. After considering the "accomplished fact," the idea of building up a town in such a delightful place appealed to Mr. Eastman, so he purchased [from William Lee] the two lots (405 acres) on both sides of the railroad tracks through Eastman, and with the assistance of a good engineer, laid out a beautiful town with wide avenues, little triangles, circles, etc.

Mr. Eastman then set out to form a new county. He drew a county of about 25 miles square, taking land from the three counties of Pulaski, Telfair and Montgomery, in such a manner that Eastman was in the center, and would therefore become the county seat. Knowing that there would be opposition from the taxpayers to the new county, since a new court house would have to be built, he went to one of the sons of William E. Dodge, then in Eastman, and made a proposal: if Mr. Dodge would build the court house on land that Mr. Eastman would donate, the new county would be named "Dodge" in his honor. This information was telegraphed off to Mr. Dodge in New York, who immediately accepted the proposition. Mr. Eastman then went to Dr. James Monroe Buchan, one of the State Representatives from Pulaski County, the county then having two, and they drew up the act to create a new county to be named Dodge. This legislation was enacted by the General Assembly and on October 26, 1870, the new county of Dodge was born. During the same session, an Act to Incorporate the Town of Eastman was approved on October 27, 1870. (Some writers claim that the town was incorporated in 1872. This is incorrect.)

The new town rapidly started to grow. In an article in the *Eastman Times* of January 31, 1873, describing the new town, the new court house, erected by Mr. J. H. Russell, Architect, under the supervision of William Pitt Eastman, had been completed at a cost of $25,000, and paid for by Mr. William E. Dodge, on land donated by Mr. Eastman. Mr. Eastman's new mansion had just been completed at a cost of $10,000. This house, now owned by the Dodge Historical Society, still stands on Eastman Way in Eastman. William E. Dodge lived in New York City. In the following year on April 4, 1874, he visited Eastman and dedicated the new court house. The dedication took place in the court house on Saturday night with a large crowd of Eastmanites in attendance. Several prominent speakers spoke after Mr. Dodge, and thanked him for the new court house. This court house was torn down in 1906 to make way for the present building which was completed in 1908. It burned in 1939 and was replaced by the current court house. The article went on to say that, of Eastman: "We have lawyers, doctors, merchants, boot and shoe maker, tanner, carpenters, bricklayers, blacksmiths, & c., but room enough for more."

Mr. Eastman's home, at the time he lived there, sat on a fifty to sixty acre plot of land that was landscaped with walk-ways, trees, flowers, greenery and exotic plants. Part of this land was used as a farm, and Mr. Eastman grew "cotton, corn, oats, cane and everything that this soil will produce," to quote the *Eastman Times*, of June 1, 1876. It was described as one of the most beautiful estates in the South. The people of Eastman were invited to use these grounds as a park, and to young couples, it was a popular place for a Sunday stroll.

Mr. Eastman, from the very start, was interested in, and supported, institutions of religion. In 1870, Miss Amalthea Foster, daughter of General Ira Foster (and soon to be Mrs. Arthur Page), started a Sunday School class of only two pupils in her own private room. The class soon swelled to twenty pupils at which time Mr. Eastman, at his own expense, erected a small comfortable house for their use. The school continued to grow and was soon organized as the Eastman Sabbath School. The school accommodated all faiths as there were no church buildings in Eastman then. Church services were held in the court house by all denominations. Mr. Eastman was a staunch supporter of the Sabbath School and held various offices within the organization. He usually taught a class, as did his daughter, Caro, and the *Eastman Times* of January 1, 1880 reported that he was elected Treasurer in the then re-named Eastman Union Sunday School. In 1885 he was elected Vice Superintendent. Even after Caro was married and lived in Macon, she would usually teach a Sabbath School class upon her frequent visits to Eastman.

Mr. Eastman donated land for all of the religious denominations of the town, both white and black. As a case in point, the *Eastman Times*, of June 11, 1874, reports that Mr. Eastman had donated eight lots of land on Bethel Street to the Methodist denomination for the purpose of erecting a church (it was quite a while before the church was built). Mr. Eastman and his family were of the Presbyterian faith, and he and his daughter, Caro, (his wife having already died), became charter members of the Eastman Presbyterian Church by letter from Presbyterian Church U.S.A., upon its organization on June 23, 1877. Mr. Eastman and J. W. Sheldon were elected Ruling Elders, and Mr. Sheldon accepted, was ordained and installed in the duties of the office. Mr. Eastman being absent at the election, apparently did not accept the appointment since there is no record of his acceptance.

Another aspect of the public life in the city that was of much interest to Mr. Eastman was the cemetery. Mr. Eastman donated the land comprising the original confines of Woodlawn Cemetery. A Board of Trustees was appointed and in March 1876, the board, through their attorneys, Messrs. L. A. Hall and J. F. DeLacy, petitioned the Superior Court of Dodge County for a charter to be incorporated under the name and style of the Woodlawn Cemetery Association for the space of twenty years. The cemetery was laid off by lots, with paths and drives, shrubbery and trees were planted and a fence erected. The lots were then made available to the public. Mr. Eastman served on the board of trustees for the remainder of his life. At a meeting of the Association on August 4, 1886, the following Trustees were elected: William Pitt Eastman, for five years, President; Charles R. Armstrong, for four years, Secretary and Treasurer; W. W. Ashburn, for three years; D. W. Weaver, for two years; and Matthew Clark, for one year. Mr. Eastman died before the expiration of his term.

During the years that he lived in Eastman, Mr. Eastman considered himself to be a real estate agent and farmer. His real estate holdings as of June 3, 1875, in the counties of Pulaski, Telfair, Dodge, Laurens and Montgomery, consisted of 225 lots of land for a total of 45,650 acres. From all available evidence, it appears that his farming was of the nature of a hobby rather than a business. He enjoyed gardening and working with plants and perhaps fancied himself to be a farmer, but since his estate in Eastman was not more than sixty acres, and after giving some of it away for the hotel and other uses, he wound up with an estate of about thirty acres. After considering the space needed for his home and extensive grounds, this did not leave much area for farming. His farming was perhaps limited to raising food for his household and his live stock. He was listed as a farmer in the 1880 census of Dodge County, and as a farmer and real estate agent in a Senate Gazetteer of Business and

Planters published in 1884. In a similar publication in 1881, he was not listed. His farming aside, he did deal in real estate, and from time to time acted as an agent for the Dodge Company.

Another enterprise to which we can identify him was the Eastman Hotel Company. On April 6, 1876, the *Eastman Times* ran a legal notice of an Application for Charter of the Eastman Hotel Company. The petitioners for this charter were A. G. P. Dodge, William Pitt Eastman, Norman W. Dodge, W. W. Ashburn, James Bishop, I. H. Russell and Henry Neiman. J. F. DeLacy was their attorney. A follow-up article dated June 1, 1876, indicated that the charter had been approved and work on the hotel had begun. A Board of Trustees had been elected and consisted of A. G. P. Dodge, N. W. Dodge, W. P. Eastman, James Bishop, and Henry Neiman. These gentlemen promptly proceeded to elect officers with the following results: William Pitt Eastman, President; A. G. P. Dodge, Treasurer; and W. F. Moss, Secretary. So far as can be determined from articles in the newspapers, Mr. Eastman retained the title of President for the remainder of his life. Mr. Eastman donated six acres of his own estate for the hotel site with the stipulation that it must always be used for that purpose (a stipulation that apparently has long since been forgotten or ignored, since a bank presently occupies that site). The hotel, named the Uplands Hotel, was designed, built, furnished and operated as a luxury facility, catering to the upper class, ostensibly people from the north. Travelers and writers praised it as being one of the finest hostelries in the country. The hotel was completed in February 1877, and the March 15, 1877, edition of the *Eastman Times*, published this short statement under the heading "Town and Country." "The Uplands is crowded with guests, and the general verdict is that 'mine host' is a good one." The hotel operated for many years through good times and bad, and with a constantly changing management. Between two and four o'clock on Sunday morning, June 9, 1907, the Uplands was completely destroyed by fire. It was not rebuilt.

Mr. Eastman loved the town of his namesake; he enjoyed his fine home and grounds, and he especially liked the climate; but almost to the end of his life he maintained a home in his old home town of Gilmanton, New Hampshire, and he and his family visited there each year, usually in the late summer, for a lengthy stay. He was in Gilmanton in 1875 when his aged mother, Mrs. Deborah Greeley Eastman, 90, died on September 12. She was in her usual good health up until the day of her death.

Mr. Eastman faced another, and his worst tragedy and it was not long in coming.

On the 17th of February, 1876, Mrs. Helena Dekay Fondey Eastman, wife of William Pitt Eastman, died at their home in Eastman. Unfortunately, the edition of the *Eastman Times* that was published on the day of her death and the one for the following week are both missing, so the details of her death are not known. Fortunately, due to public demand for additional copies, her obituary was reprinted in the March 2, 1876 edition of the *Times*. The obituary is interesting in that it gives some insight in the death and funeral of a person of the upper class to the Eastman of the 1870's and is, therefore included herein as an appendix. Mrs. Eastman was buried on their estate in Eastman, but her remains were later removed to Woodlawn Cemetery, after the establishment of that place.

After the death of Mrs. Eastman, Mr. Eastman and his only living child, Caro, did considerable traveling, mostly to Macon and Savannah and often to New York, and they still made their annual trip to Gilmanton. In a letter written by Mr. Eastman in 1881 he indicated that he had sold the old home in Gilmanton, but he and his daughter still made their annual visit, apparently staying in Center Harbor, a small town in the same county (Belknap County) as Gilmanton.

The *Eastman Times* of August 1, 1878, had this notice under the heading, "Local News," "Mr. Wm. Pitt Eastman and his accomplished daughter, Miss Caro, left here on Friday morning for a short visit to New Hampshire. We wish them a safe return." The edition of August 29, had this notice: "Mrs. Ogden will please accept our thanks for a nice piece of wedding cake, received by mail in good order, from Gilmanton, New Hampshire." This presented somewhat of a mystery until seeing the August 25, 1878, edition of the *Macon Telegraph and Messenger,* which announced that Mr. James Monroe Ogden of that city (Macon), was married on the 22nd of August, 1878, to Miss Caro C. Eastman, daughter of the Honorable William Pitt Eastman, in Gilmanton, New Hampshire. After a honeymoon in New England, the Ogdens returned to Macon to live, where Mr. Ogden was an important insurance executive with Turpin, Ogden & Co. The Ogdens lived at 274 Georgia Avenue in that city. Mrs. Ogden, while living in Macon, made frequent visits to her father in Eastman, and he likewise visited her often. The Ogden's had three daughters, Helena Eastman Ogden, born August 26, 1879; Caro Eastman Ogden, born December 1882; and Susan Eastman Ogden, born May 21, 1884. Little Caro lived only seven weeks and died February 12, 1883. Her remains were brought to her grandfather's house in

Eastman, and after her funeral, she was buried in Woodlawn Cemetery.

After the marriage of his daughter, Mr. Eastman continued with his activities in Eastman. He was concerned about the appearance of the town. He saw to the landscaping of the Uplands Hotel and planted Japan Wax trees around the courthouse. When some of these died he personally replaced them. He continued to work with the cemetery, churches and schools. In 1885 he became Mayor of Eastman and served one term. By this time his health was getting worse and the *Eastman Times* of January 21, 1886, under the heading of "Local Short Stops," had this notice: "The many friends of Hon. Wm. Pitt Eastman will be glad to learn that he is convalescing rapidly at the home of his daughter, Mrs. J. Monroe Ogden, in Macon, where he is receiving the best medical attention and all the comforts that loving hands can administer. We hope for a speedy and complete recovery of his wonted excellent health." And in the April 1, 1886, edition: "We are pleased to state that Hon. W. P. Eastman is again able to appear on our streets.

In the late summer of 1888, the Honorable William Pitt Eastman made his final trip to New Hampshire. He and his daughter, Caro, were in Center Harbor on their annual visit when he died, with her by his side, on September 2,

1888. He was 75 years old. The newspapers (*Eastman Times* and after August 1888, the *Times-Journal*, from May 1887 through January 1889) are missing, so we are unable to get the immediate reaction of the people in Eastman at the news of Mr. Eastman's death, we do, however, have items from newspapers in nearby counties:

The *Montgomery Monitor*, September 12, 1888: DEATH OF WM. PITT EASTMAN. "Hon. William Pitt Eastman, founder of the town of Eastman, Georgia, died at Center Harbor, New Hampshire on the 2d instant. He had gone on a visit to his former home when he died. He was in his 75th year, and was a member of the Presbyterian Church. He was a public spirited and useful citizen, and greatly beloved by all who knew him."

The *Hawkinsville Dispatch*, September 6, 1888: DEATH of MR. EASTMAN. The Founder of the Town of Eastman Dies in New Hampshire. "The *Telegraph's* Eastman correspondent sends this news which will be read with regret by many who knew Mr. Eastman. A telegram from Center Harbor, New Hampshire, announces the death of Hon. Wm. Pitt Eastman, who was spending his summer with his daughter, Mrs. J. Monroe Ogden and her children of your city. The sad intelligence cast a gloom over our whole community; while we knew that Mr. Eastman's health was frail and precarious, we were not expecting to hear of his sudden death. No man was more universally respected in this section, and no man contributed more toward the progress and development of our county than did he. Eastman was his special pride and our town and community have lost one of its best men.

"Appropriate ceremonies will be had by the town and its institutions. The remains will be temporarily interred where he died, but we presume in a short time he will be buried here by the side of his beloved wife and child."

The *Macon Telegraph and Messenger*, September 4, 1888, printed the same article as did the Hawkinsville paper.

A handwritten paper provided by Faye Sheffield Jessup, of Eastman, Georgia, reads as follows:

DEATH OF HON. WILLIAM PITT EASTMAN

"The sad news of the death of this grand old gentleman, of our town, reached us on Monday last, and cast a pall of gloom over our entire community. Mr. Eastman, at the time of his demise, was visiting his old home at Center Harbor, N. H., accompanied by his daughter, Mrs. J. Monroe Ogden, who was beside him when his spirit took flight.

The subject of this sketch was the founder of our town, for whom it was named, and had resided here almost continuously for the past 15 or 16 years.

To say that the deceased was beloved here is putting it all too mildly. He was universally beloved and esteemed, and many are the hearts now bowed in at his death. Mr. Eastman was in his 75th year, a member of the Presbyterian Church, and during his sojourn among us he had led a quiet, unobtrusive life, a life exemplary of the true Christian.

His remains are temporally interred at Center Harbor, and will probably be exhumed in the near future and interred here or in Macon.

A good man has fallen—peace to his ashes.

Sept 1st 1888."

The above note was most likely a copy of the obituary of Mr. Eastman from the *Times-Journal*, written by Mr. M. L. Burch, the Editor. The article is written in his exact style as well as his terminology. The term "peace to his ashes" seemed to be a favorite of Mr. Burch since he often used it.

Also from Mrs. Jessup, we have the following clipping, most likely from the September 6, 1888, edition of the *Times-Journal*:

CITIZENS MEETING
Resolution in Memory of
Wm. Pitt Eastman

EASTMAN, Ga., Sept. 5, 1888.

In pursuance of the call issued by Mayor Bishop, the citizens of Eastman met in the court house this day for the purpose of paying an appropriate tribute of respect to the memory of our honored fellow citizen, WILLIAM PITT EASTMAN, who died at Center Harbor, New Hampshire, last Sunday night. Jas. Bishop, Jr. was elected chairman, and R. J. Stozier, secretary. The secretary was requested to read the resolutions given below, on behalf of Mr. J. F. DeLacy, who was absent from town. The resolutions were seconded by Messrs. L. A. Hall, Henry Coleman, R. D. Gentry, Dr. H. Fisher, Jas. Bishop, Jr., and R. J. Stozier, all of whom spoke feelingly of the exemplary life and character and many good deeds of MR. EASTMAN, and of the great loss sustained in his death. The resolutions were then unanimously adopted.

On motion of Dr. Fisher, a resolution was adopted that a committee be appointed to inform Mrs. J. M. Ogden that it is the desire of the people that the body of MR. EASTMAN be brought to Eastman for permanent interment, if consistent with her wishes, and that they will be pleased to co-operate with her in the matter. Dr. H. Fisher, J. F. DeLacy and R. J. Stozier were appointed on that committee.

RESOLUTIONS

The people of Eastman have heard with profound regret of the death of their honored friend and fellow-citizen, WILLIAM PITT EASTMAN, and have assembled in public meeting for the purpose of giving expression to their sincere regret and the esteem in which he was uniformly held by all classes of our people.

But a short while since our venerable friend was among us—inquiring about public affairs, and suggesting ways and means to promote the welfare and prosperity of the town which bears his name.

When we consider what a factor for good and what an agent for the public weal we had in him; how much he contributed by work and deed towards the development of Eastman, its churches, its schools, its businesses and its institutions; how much individual work he did, and his lavish expenditure of money to make Eastman the foremost town in this section; when we think of all these things, we feel how feeble is the attempt to portray a character so completely rounded and so perfectly adapted to the conditions surrounding him, and we deeply deplore the great and irreparable loss we sustain in his death. As a fitting and appropriate tribute to his worth as a man and citizen, be it

Resolved, That in the death of MR. EASTMAN our town and county have sustained an irremediable loss; that our institutions have been deprived of one of their best and wisest members, and that his name and memory will be perpetuated by those who survive him.

Resolved, That we extend to his beloved daughter, Mrs. J. Monroe (Caro) Ogden, our heartfelt sympathy and condolence, and give her assurance of our earnest friendship.

Unanimously adopted, September 5, 1888

    Jas. Bishop, Jr., Chairman
    R. J. Stozier, Secretary

BURIAL IN WOODLAWN CEMETERY

Mr. Eastman was interred temporarily in the cemetery at Center Harbor, New Hampshire. Sometime during the year in 1889, Mr. Eastman's remains were removed from Center Harbor to the Woodlawn Cemetery in Eastman, Georgia.

LAST WILL AND TESTAMENT

Mr. Eastman died *testate* and his will was simplicity itself, as evidenced by the following:

I, William Pitt Eastman, being of sound and disposing mind to make this my last will and testament.

I give, devise and bequeath all of my property, real, personal, and mixed to my daughter, Caro C. Eastman, absolutely. I name and appoint my daughter, Caro. C. Eastman, sole executrix for this my last will and testament and I recommend that she consult and advise with my friend, Charles A. Peabody, as her legal advisor in matters connected with my estate.

I authorize my executrix to sell and convey any or all of my real estate, and I request that she may not be required to give bonds for the faithful performance of her interest as executrix.

In witness whereof I have hereto affixed by seal and signed my name this 16th day of November 1877.

WILLIAM PITT EASTMAN'S GRANDAUGHTER VISITS EASTMAN IN 1951

His daughter, Mrs. Ogden, petitioned for probate to the Ordinary of Dodge County on October 26th, 1888. Her attorneys were J. F. DeLacy and James Bishop, Jr. The disposition of the estate took many years and as late as 1904, Mrs. Ogden was still selling off land in Dodge and nearby counties. The Eastman home was rented out for a time and was eventually sold. The house was sold in 1992 to the Dodge Historical Society by Mrs. Cary Bullock.

After the death of her husband, James Monroe Ogden, on March 10, 1901, Mrs. Caro Eastman Ogden and her two daughters, Helena and Susie, moved to New York City. Mrs. Ogden died there on July 8, 1929. Her remains were interred in the Rose Hill Cemetery in Macon, Georgia, beside her husband. Her daughter, Susan Eastman Ogden, died without having been married and was buried at Ferncliff Cemetery, Hartsdale, New York.

Her remaining daughter, Helena Eastman Ogden, after receiving her education at private schools and Wesleyan College, graduating there in 1897, married Rev. R. J. Campbell in 1906. They had one child, Mary Eastman Campbell. Helena was an outstanding portrait painter and won many honors for her work.

On Sunday, June 3, 1951, Mrs. Campbell and her daughter, Mary, visited Eastman. It was Mrs. Campbell's only visit to Eastman since she was eight years old. The Campbell's were escorted about the town by Attorney D. D. Smith, who had met them that morning at the post office. They saw the old Eastman home and visited Ogden Avenue which had been named for Mrs. Campbell's mother, Caro. C. Eastman Ogden. They visited the court house and viewed the plaque placed there by the DAR in honor of Mr. Eastman and Mr. Dodge, the inscription which reads:

"In Appreciation of the Gift by William Pitt Eastman and William E. Dodge of the Former Court House and the Grounds on Which This Building Stands. This Tablet is Placed by the Col. William Few Chapter, DAR 1916."

At the city park [adjacent to the old Library building on Fifth Avenue] they saw the marker erected in 1916 by the Woman's Club in honor of Mr. Eastman. The inscription of the marker reads:

"In honor of William Pitt Eastman, philanthropist and Christian, founder and benefactor of the City of Eastman, where he spent the last years of his life endearing himself to the people, who fully appreciate his generosity, benevolence and charity."

Mrs. Campbell had promised her mother many years before that she would paint a portrait of her grandfather, William Pitt Eastman, and present it to the town of Eastman. She was finally able to complete the painting and it was presented to the town on May 7, 1954. The painting was unveiled by Linda Smith, great granddaughter of Mr. and Mrs. E. A. Smith, who had known the Eastman's. The portrait was accepted for the city by Bob Wright, the City Manager and D. D. Smith gave an interesting talk at the ceremony. The portrait of Mr. Eastman, formerly held by the Dodge County Library, now hangs in the Eastman House. [Note the following article from the *Eastman Times-Journal* regarding the painting.]

Mrs. Campbell's daughter, Mary Eastman Campbell, was married on December 26, 1962, to William E. Flannery of New York City. Mr. Flannery was an attorney with the firm of DeWitt, Nast, and Diskin, of New York City. The Flannerys had no children, thus terminating the descent of William Pitt Eastman.

Helena Eastman Ogden Campbell, portrait painter and writer, died on March 30, 1964, at Lawrence Hospital, Bronxville, New York. She was buried at Ferncliff Cemetery, Hartsdale, New York. Her only survivor was her daughter, Mary Eastman Campbell Flannery.

Any story about Eastman and the Eastman family would be incomplete without mentioning Mrs. James M. Arthur. Mrs. Arthur, the former Mary Helen Willcox, born February 27, 1857, and died September 7, 1950, knew the Eastmans well. Her second child, Caro Eastman Arthur, born November 18, 1877, and died October 29, 1888, was named for Mr. Eastman's daughter, Caro. The child died of scarlet fever and lies buried in Woodlawn Cemetery with her mother and father. Mrs. Arthur lived to a very old age and related many stories about the early days of Eastman, since her husband was a pioneer settler of the town, and she had lived there since 1873.

Lot No. 258 is designated the W. P. Eastman lot on the map of Woodlawn Cemetery, Eastman, Georgia. There is not, however, a single marker or monument in that lot. We have documentary evidence that Mr. Eastman, his wife, daughter, and granddaughter, are buried there. The lack of markers or monuments in the lot, for a man as wealthy as Mr. Eastman, remains a mystery. John D. Willcox, at his own initiative, has completed restoration of the lot and has installed an appropriate monument to Mr. Eastman and the other members of his family buried there. This work was completed in February 1991.

Standing at this point in time, the year 1991, and looking back over the history of Eastman and Dodge County, it becomes abundantly clear that no man has contributed as much to the town and county as did the Honorable William Pitt Eastman. He was one Yankee that came South after the Civil War and left more than he took away.

WILLIAM PITT EASTMAN PORTRAIT

The Times-Journal
Eastman, Georgia, Wednesday, May 12, 1954

SMITH TALK AT UNVEILING OF WM. P. EASTMAN PORTRAIT

The following is the complete text of the talk given by D. D. Smith Friday afternoon [May 7, 1954] at the unveiling of the portrait of Mr. William Pitt Eastman at the Dodge County Library. The painting was unveiled by Linda Lee Smith, granddaughter of Mr. Smith.

"One Sunday morning last spring I noticed two nice looking ladies in an automobile parked in front of the post office. They seemed to want some information and upon engaging in conversation with them it was not long before I discovered that I had met the granddaughter and great-granddaughter of the Honorable William Pitt Eastman.

"Their time was limited but they were interested in seeing Ogden Avenue, the old Eastman home, the city park, and the court house and it was my privilege and pleasure to point out these places to them. They had a very brief visit in my home with my mother who, in the early days of Eastman, knew Mr. Eastman and his wife. These two ladies were Mrs. Helena Ogden Campbell and her daughter, Miss Mary Campbell.

"In June following their visit to Eastman I received a letter from Mrs. Campbell that I think you will find interesting":

"Dear Mr. Smith:

"Years ago I promised my mother that I would paint a portrait of my grandfather for Eastman. She wrote to the Women's Club (that had shared in erecting the monument to him) and they enthusiastically received the idea, wished to make arrangements for hanging the portrait. But it was not as of yet painted! Through the intervening years there have been many times I have taken up the proposition, but first one thing and then another have prevented my finishing the work.

"The portrait is now ready. It is small—just the head—on canvas 20 x 24, and has a hand carved frame.

"As your mother knew my grandfather, would you care to be the one to receive the picture and see if there be a place in the Court House where it could hang (or some other appropriate spot, if any?) And is your mother strong enough to "unveil the portrait?"

"If for any reason you do not care to do this, please be quite frank about it and I will communicate with someone else. But, naturally, I thought first of you.

"Several weeks ago, I sent you a notice of an exhibition I am now having in New York City. The portrait is in that show and so would not be available until that closes the end of June. After that, it would be shipped to Eastman, preferably in the fall.

"With regards to you and your mother.

Sincerely,
H. E. Ogden Campbell"

"Of course, I wrote to Mrs. Campbell and told her that we would be glad to receive the portrait and see that it was hung in some appropriate place. She shipped the portrait several months after the letter was written and then we further postponed hanging it because the library had not been completely finished and we thought this would be the most appropriate place for it.

"Mr. Eastman, as many of you know, was among the earliest and first citizens of Eastman, having come here in 1870. He and his wife, at one time, were members of the Eastman Presbyterian church. He was intimately identified, not only with the religious life of the community, but in many other respects. He served as mayor of our town in the year 1885, and the records show he was a member of the local Masonic Lodge, having joined in 1879. Mr. Eastman was well to do financially and proved to be a benefactor, indeed, of our city in its early days, evidences of his liberality even now surrounding us. He generously donated the land for the new town and county seat, the land where the court house now stands, the Woodlawn cemetery property, the city park property on which this library building is located, had built and presented to Eastman its first school house in 1873, and he donated the land for the construction of a number of churches in our county.

"While our town is rather young for history, one of the historic places intimately connected with Mr. Eastman is the house now occupied by Mr. and Mrs. Cary Bullock [as of 1954] and family on Eastman Way. It was built and occupied by Mr. Eastman with his family, and Mrs. Campbell, his granddaughter, was born there. In Mr. Eastman's day it was the center of a large tract of 30 acres, with attractive drives, imposing trees, beautiful shrubbery and gorgeous flowers.

"Mrs. Campbell, as stated, was born there, but moved away when she was only 8 years old. She was a member of the Class of 1897 at Wesleyan College where she studied art, and she is today an artist of wide reputation. She has won national recognition as a portrait painter. Among her portraits is a group of Columbia University professors, including Dr. Henry Carr Pearson, Dr. William H. Kirkpatrick, Dr. Gustave L. Van Roosbroeck and Dr. Julia Haskell, as well as the portrait of the Rev. George F. Nelson, Canon of the Cathedral of St. John the Divine, and last but by no means least, to those who know him, a portrait of Dr. William F. Quillian, which hangs in the Alumnae office at Wesleyan.

"In 1932 Mrs. Campbell was inspired to gather from well known contemporary artists representative works of art for Wesleyan College, and the present collection, including paintings, etchings, and statuary, totals about 140. Mrs. Campbell lives at present with her daughter, Miss Mary Campbell, who was with her on her visit to Eastman last year, and who is a person of prominence in her own right. She is executive secretary of Conde Nast Publications, serves as Personnel Director for the company, and also as Job Editor for Glamour Magazine. In 1951 she was asked to be the alumnae day speaker at Wesleyan College, her mother's alma mater. We are more glad that Mrs. Campbell's mother commissioned her many years ago to paint this portrait of her grandfather, a man whose memory should and will be ever dear to our people, and it is with a feeling of distinct honor and pleasure that I present Mrs. Campbell on this occasion in now presenting the portrait on her behalf to the people of Eastman."

WILLIAM PITT EASTMAN LETTER

[Note: This letter prepared by Mr. Eastman to provide biographical details for publication in a local history of his hometown area, in Gilmanton, New Hampshire.]

Eastman, Ga. Oct. 4th 1881
Capt. Wm. Badger,

My dear sir,

You may have heard that I was in N.H. last month. I felt very desirous to see you and had I known that you were to be there, I would have postponed leaving for a few days, but only until the stage was entering Belmont, was I informed by the driver, that you arrived the night before. This was on Friday having my daughter, child and nurse with me, on our way to New York to take the steamer for Savannah on Saturday morning our passage and rooms being engaged. The stage took us to your house that I might have a moment with you, but we failed to find you. I wish to know when your "History of Gilmanton" is to be published, and also whether you received from me a statement of my life and whether any notice of it will appear in your book. I read in the little paper of Gilmanton an account of my brother Arthur's life, in which my own life was intimately connected, he commenced business at the academy village and I at the iron works. I bought out Moses P. Page in 1836, remained there two years, built a store that is now occupied there. I was successful so went and joined my brother in an enterprise that took us to the western part of Missouri and Arkansas a very eventful trip, at our time we were left for weeks high up in the Arkansas River, the river having fallen too low for steamers, and we with our hands, made a flat boat, put in our trunks and pulled that boat two miles to Little Rock, taking 4 days and 5 nights, one in the stern to steer and the other paddling and taking turns. After reaching home via New Orleans and by stages, no railroads, we founded the firm of A.M. & W.P. Eastman and went into the grocery and foreign fruit business in Boston and subsequently took in a partner and added Commission of Western Produce, made and lost large sums of money. We were full partners for eight years and dissolved and operated separately, most of the time after but we never had any difficulty or disagreement and we continued to act and feel toward each other as brothers should, until he was suddenly taken from us. I then had the satisfaction of having his body brought to our old house and a funeral at the house and placed his remains in the new cemetery and in the spot selected by him and pointed out to me just one year before, while we were placing the family monuments. He was then enjoying perfect health, but he was adamant in expressing his desire that a particular corner of the lot be reserved for himself and wife.

We always assisted each other in our enterprises, loaning money, our notes or endorsements, never refusing. At the time of his struggling to complete his great enterprise, the "Direct Cable," he had six thousand dollars of my money for some years, which he returned and then invested in Georgia a few thousand with me, and had he lived would undoubtedly have been largely interested here. The first enterprise that I entered into, after leaving Boston, was to get up a large knitting establishment, located at Newark, N.J. Formed a joint stock company with a cash capital of 200,000, paid in. I directed the getting up the whole affair and had full charge of it for twelve years, making the best of ladies and gents underwear, that has ever been made in our country. My monument is still standing there being the largest building in the city and in operation making money, being now 21 years since I left it. I then visited England and France twice. Spent in all two years in Paris obtaining valuable ideas in the manufacturing of goods. In 1862 I was induced to visit the Pine Forest of Georgia and to examine a tract of 300,000 acres of the best quality of yellow pine timber, located in the center of Georgia which had been owned for many years by gentlemen residing in New York, Boston, Philadelphia and Baltimore, and after spending much time in examining the proper titles, I returned and obtained control of the entire property. The property having been inaccessible until now about to be opened by the Macon and Brunswick R.R. I formed a joint stock company, called it the Georgia Land and Lumber Company, and put in 200,000 acres, at half million dollars. Hon. Wm. E. Dodge and family of N.Y. bought a controlling interest and finally all of the stock and then purchased of me 100,000 acres more, so that they now owned 300,000 acres and are manufacturing sixty million feet of lumber per year. I had in the mean time purchased about 50,000 acres more, which I still have and which is daily increasing in value. In my absence in Europe with my family in 1871, I received in London, a letter from Mr. Hazlehurst, President of the Macon and Brunswick R.R. stating that they had finished the road and had formed and numbered stations every ten miles and already given to some of them names and that he had taken the liberty to name station No. 13, Eastman for me, "it being the

Early Citizens of Dodge County 39

place, of all others on the road, for a town," the highest land & c. It did not strike me favorably for I knew that if I accepted it, they would expect me to spend money, so I thanked him for the compliment and declined the honor. I wrote to another person to prevent it, but after some five months I returned and found that they had put the name on the train depot and after visiting the place and examining a view of becoming interested in the building of a town, I found it to be a delightful healthy place, pleasant climate, summer and winter, pure air and excellent water, about 600 feet above the ocean, dry air and good soil, so I accepted and became interested, took 2 lots 405 acres on both sides of the R.R. and with the assistance of a good engineer, we laid out a beautiful town, avenues 70 feet for the drive, sidewalks and trees. Little triangles, circles, *and c* [etc]. were made. I selected a mound of 60 acres, upon which I placed our buildings, ground that had been cultivated.

I planned the forming of Dodge Co. by taking from 4 other counties in which our land lie, making a county of 25 miles square, and having my town in its center, having said nothing to anyone, I considered the causes of the opposition that I might meet with, one of which was, that those coming into the new county would be taxed to building public buildings. This I said to one of Mr. Dodge's sons and that if their family would build for us a good court house, we would call the county Dodge. The son was pleased and the father was written to and he consented and I carried the case through the Legislature and had the new county of Dodge made. Mr. Dodge immediately ordered a court house built, costing some $15,000, Eastman becoming the county town and is in the center of the county.

Our town is becoming a favorite place of resort in winter by the north and western people. Our "Uplands Hotel" is a very superior house for the south, well kept by a northern man, cost some $65,000. We have an academy, "Eastman Academy," charter and by-laws copied from those of Gilmanton. Have a good two story building, male and female teachers and 70 scholars, churches, 8 or 10 stores, a newspaper, lumber mills and naval stores and c [etc].

When I began this letter I intended merely to ask about the book, if not too late, with your advice, to make something prepared, as it did not appear quite the thing to have so much said about my dear brother and nothing about his brother, who has equaled him, as he would say, in every act of his life. The Ga. Operation which will carry to the end of time, excels the cable enterprise, which already has its equal.

The Macon and Brunswick Road is 185 miles long, this town is 132 miles north of Brunswick and 56 miles south of Macon and is the highest land on the road. It is now 10 years since I have considered it my home. In 1839, I married my wife, Helena D. Fondey of Albany, N.Y. We had two daughters, Helena T. and Caro C. Helena died at the age of twenty. Caro married August 1878, Mr. J. Monroe Ogden of Macon, Ga. and now resides there, has a daughter, Helena Eastman, two years old, so I am quite alone here. My daughter and granddaughter are two hours by rail from me, so that we are often together. Being about 12 hundred miles from our old home in Gilmanton and where neither of us could be there more than a few weeks in a year and at a great expense. We felt it better to let it go and are glad to know friends are to own it. Now should you ever review this and have the time patience to use it, please let me know whether anything can be done with it and what. Can you sift over, preserve and shape something readable out of it and if you publish it how shall I compensate you?

Your Friend

Wm. Pitt Eastman

Should anything be printed let it appear as if written by someone who knew both brothers. If Judge Ira Eastman were alive, he would do me justice.

(Editorial Note: Grammar, text, and punctuation retained as shown in the copy provided)

June 1994

JUDGE JAMES BISHOP, Sr.

The life of Judge James Bishop, Sr. is closely connected with the growth and development of Eastman, Georgia, and the surrounding country. He was born in Pulaski County December 1, 1829. We associate the name of Judge Bishop with the Eastman House because he lived there during his productive years.

The father of Judge James Bishop, Sr. was Simeon Bishop (1799-1836), a native of New Jersey. Simeon moved south as a young man to superintend a large lumber business near Darien, Georgia, but later made his home in the southern part of Pulaski County where he conducted a large mercantile business. He married Nancy J. Daniel who died in 1873. Simeon, Nancy and their son, John, are buried in the original family burial ground called Englewood.

James Bishop was the second son of Simeon and Nancy Daniel. James married Mary E. Guyton in 1853. She was the daughter of Major Moses Guyton, a prominent Laurens County citizen. Mary Bishop was a well-educated person, speaking and mastering five different languages. She was a member of the First Methodist Church, organized the first Foreign Missionary and Home

Missionary Society called the Dorcas Society. Mrs. Bishop was born July 7, 1833, and died December 18, 1888. She and James Bishop, her husband, are buried in the Bishop Lot in Woodlawn Cemetery, Eastman, Georgia.

Soon after the end of the Civil War that part of Pulaski County where James Bishop lived was cut off to help form the new county of Dodge with Eastman as the county seat. Judge Bishop, foreseeing the future possibilities of the new town, moved there while it was in its infancy. He was the second mayor of the town, succeeding General Ira R. Foster. He was a charter member of the Eastman Lodge of the Masonic Order. He was Judge of the County Court, County School Commissioner for twelve years and wrote the first charter and incorporation papers for the town of Eastman. Judge Bishop and Mr. Eastman were friends of many years standing and Judge Bishop purchased the Eastman House from Caro Eastman Ogden in the early 1890s to use as his home.

James Bishop and his wife had eight children, three sons and five daughters. Only one son lived to maturity and he was James Bishop, Jr., born March 31, 1857, died February 20, 1908. Their first daughter was Mary who married G.F. Harrison; the second daughter, Helen, lived in Eastman at the family home; the third daughter died early in life; the fourth daughter, Carolyn, married R.L.

Bush of North Carolina and the youngest daughter, Estelle, married Ellis Way Bullock, a native of North Carolina.

James Bishop, Jr., married Mannie Douglas of Talbotton, Georgia. He studied law at the University of Georgia and was a partner under the firm name of DeLacy and Bishop. He died at 50 years of age.

May 1995

WILLIAM EARL DODGE

Our county was named Dodge by William Pitt Eastman for his friend, William Earl Dodge. The county was created by an Act of the General Assembly on October 26, 1870, and the land was taken from Pulaski, Montgomery, and Telfair counties. Mr. Dodge expressed his appreciation of the honor conferred on him by having built at his own expense a magnificent court house and presented it to the citizens of the county. It was erected where the present court house now stands and was a two-story frame structure which cost about $25,000.

William E. Dodge was a New Englander by birth and a merchant by training. At the age of thirteen he worked as a junior clerk at the store of a friendly but exacting New York Quaker. After finishing his apprenticeship with the Quaker storekeeper, young Dodge assisted his father in the dry goods business until he opened a store of his own in New York in 1827. In 1828, he married Melissa Phelps, the daughter of Anson Phelps. The two families were fundamentally alike, bred in the English Puritan tradition. A family enterprise, Phelps Dodge, was soon organized and became a company of large proportions. It built factories and organized railroads, converted great forests into lumber and operated coal and iron mines. Much of the iron, copper and tin plate industry was under its control. The company became one of the largest copper fabricating companies in the United States.

Dodge had great interest in railroads and not wholly of a financial character. He believed that the cultural development of the United States depended on the large scale expansion of rail transportation. Dodge was elected a director of the Erie Railroad in 1854. He retained his position until 1857 until a split with his fellow directors over the question of running trains on Sunday which he strongly opposed on religious grounds.

In addition to large holdings in railroads and coal mines, Dodge found a large and highly profitable business in the virgin timber lands of Pennsylvania. His wide knowledge of the timber resources of the country and large profits led Dodge to extend his holdings into a number of other states and even into Canada.

In Georgia the company's lumber operations were almost on a par with those in Pennsylvania. Dodge had the advantage of long contact with the south and firsthand knowledge of much of the country from extensive travel and was deeply interested both in the problems and the opportunities.

After 1865 the Macon and Brunswick Railroad of Georgia was organized and the road ran directly through the middle of the yellow pine forest, making the rich source of lumber more accessible. A company, Georgia Land and Lumber Company, was formed and it purchased 300,000 acres of yellow pine land in 1868. The owners included not only William E. Dodge but his sons, A.G.P., George E., Norman W. and friends, William Chauncey and William Pitt Eastman. Eastman later sold his holdings and concentrated on other interests which included the establishment of the City of Eastman.

In 1878 a new Georgia law necessitated a change and the Georgia Land and Lumber Company transferred all its holdings to George E. Dodge, son of William E. In time Anson Dodge, a younger brother of George E. took over the management of the Georgia lumber business. He later became a resident of St. Simons Island.

William E. Dodge reached the end of his long and notable life in 1883 at the age of 78. He was a very religious man and always put the welfare of his fellow man first. It is said he gave away an average of a thousand dollars a day during the later years of his life. A speech is recorded by William E. Dodge in 1875 to the U.S. President and fellow citizens on behalf of the south and pleading the administration to leave the imposed legislation of the southern states to the states and let them resolve their problems themselves. Mr. Dodge had an empathy for all people.

A. G. WILLIAMSON DIED FRIDAY NIGHT

Thursday, December 10, 1925 (Newspaper Report)

Hon. A. G. Williamson, for fifty years one of Dodge County's most prominent citizens, died at his home in the city Friday night about nine o'clock, following an illness of more than a year, during which time he was practically an invalid.

Mr. Williamson's body was embalmed by J. W. Peacock Co., undertakers, and according to instructions previously given by him, was deposited in a vault at Orphans Cemetery at sundown Sunday afternoon. This vault, above which rested life-size statues of Mr. Williamson, Mrs. Williamson and J. Gould Williamson, a nephew and adopted son, was erected by Mr. Williamson about fifteen years ago, and full directions were given by him as to the disposal of his body at death. The body, lying on the left side, reposed on a cedar cot, which had also been provided by Mr. Williamson and in this position was deposited in the vault. The funeral service, which was conducted by Rev. Frank Adams, of the Christian church, consisted only of scripture reading, prayer, and two songs. The scripture was from the 14th chapter of St. John, the second to fourth verses, inclusive. The songs, "I Shall Know Him" and "Asleep in Jesus," were rendered by a double quartet composed of O.V. Lashley, Henry Manley, Robert Bennett, Mrs. Jeter A. Harrell, S.H. Goolsby, H.E. Dickens, John Parkerson, Mrs. C.F. Coleman. The active pallbearers were the following: W. Fitzgerald, W. H. Smith, C. F. Coleman, C. H. Peacock, R. G. P. McKinnon, C. C. Burch. An honorary escort composed of C. D. Phillips, W. J. Deffinall, C. B. Murrell, J. H. Rogers, W. W. Puett, J. C. Wall. The floral offerings were banked about the mausoleum in abundant profusion and were magnificently beautiful. A throng of about one thousand people was in attendance.

Mr. Williamson was born in Columbus County, N.C., and was 71 years old August 1. He came to Dodge County 52 years ago and secured employment as woods-rider for Coleman & Sessoms, a naval stores firm. Soon afterwards he was married to Miss Mattie Buchan, daughter of Dr. James Buchan by whom he is survived. Being a man of keen and accurate judgment, he early realized the value of lands in this section of Georgia, and through this judgment and his untiring energy, he acquired as the years went by 8,000 acres of Dodge County land, also large holdings in Eastman city property and government bonds. His estate is valued at between $400,000 and a half million dollars. Several months ago he deeded a large part of his property to relatives, his wife and adopted son being the principal beneficiaries.

Mr. Williamson united with the Christian church when quite a young man, and as long as his health would permit, took a very active interest in its affairs. He built the Christian church at Orphans and was an important factor in the erection of the Christian church in Eastman. To both of these institutions he was a strong pillar and liberal contributor.

Mr. Williamson was Ordinary of Dodge County two terms, beginning about 1895. His administration of this office was marked by splendid efficiency and admirable economy. He rendered to the people the same fine business management that characterized his personal affairs.

Mr. Williamson's life and character constitute a remarkable demonstration of what a man may accomplish through the exercise of economy, energy and industry, coupled with the practice of that rigid honesty and justice that marked all of his transactions.

In addition to his wife, Mr. Williamson is survived by three brothers, Messrs. R. G. and Milton, of this county, and Mr. J. L. Williamson, of Cerro Gordo, N.C.; also quite a number of nieces and nephews.   March 1997

HOMES, HOTELS AND OTHER BUILDINGS

THE EASTMAN-BISHOP-BULLOCK HOME

The cornerstone of Eastman is the Eastman-Bishop-Bullock Home. The house was built about 1870 by William Pitt Eastman for his residence.

The history of this house started with Mr. Eastman in 1870. Carol Eastman Ogden, the daughter and heir of Mr. Eastman, sold the house to Judge James Bishop. Judge Bishop died in 1920 and his daughter, Mary Helen, inherited the place. When she died in 1942 she left the house jointly to Cary Bullock and James Bishop, Jr. Cary bought out James' share in 1946 and the house has been the Bullock home since then.

The original house now stands; however, a rear house of the same architecture connected to the main house by a long latticed porch was moved to the present Presbyterian Church site. This rear house, which had the original kitchen on the first floor and servant quarters on the second floor, burned.

There is a full basement beneath the main house which once included a well and a generously sized root cellar.

The copper sink in the kitchen had a pump connected to the well in the basement. The well has now been filled in and the root cellar is not in use. There were many ingenious devices in this house which brought comfort and convenience to the occupants.

The outside front walls are cedar boards and the boards on the back are heart pine. The interior has plaster walls and eleven-foot ceilings and three-foot wainscoting of lustrous heart pine. The same lovely pine was used for the six-inch board floors. The two interior stylish staircases are of walnut and there are three marble mantles.

Mr. Eastman purchased the living room carpet from Marseilles, France, and it remained on the floor for more than a century. A rug had been used over the carpet. A sample of the carpet was used by a company that manufactured a replacement carpet that closely matched the original. This occurred in the late 1990s. The narrow guided cornice boards have been in continuous use on the living room windows.

This is a distinctive nine-room house, trimmed with the typical gingerbread on the outside. There are eight exterior entrances with three being on the front. The roof is an original copper roof and has never been in need of replacement.

Originally the entrance drive was from Main Street (along the railroad), up to the house, then circling back to Main Street. The present narrow street, known as Eastman Way, directly in front of the house, is part of the original drive. Elm and cedar trees which were on each side of the drive are still standing. There are also some of the original shrubs such as camellia bushes and pomegranate bushes growing in the gardens.

October 1993

EASTMAN HOUSE PROGRESS REPORT

The Dodge Historical society has been active since early 1993 in an effort to settle into the Eastman House and, in the process, also creating a special place for the citizens of the County to utilize the space while also offering a visitor attraction.

The home was purchased from Sarah I. Bullock in October, 1993, and the first priority has been to clean and empty the house and to improve the yard. Currently the house is useable at the first floor level and the following is a summary of accomplishments to date.

Library—The first floor is varnished and the walls are painted. The magnificent cabinets which were given by Gene and Mimi Dennis are situated and filled with donated historical items. A most interesting reproduction of a chandelier of that era has been hung. The red-cushioned cane back furniture, which consists of a sofa and two chairs, was purchased at the estate sale.

Foyer—This is a handsome area with freshly painted walls and varnished floors. The staircase, newel posts and bannisters, constitute a focal point for visitors to observe.

Living Room—This room is especially attractive with the new carpet. The color and design of the carpet is very bright with flowers but matches samples of the old carpet brought from France about 125 years ago. The handsome framed picture over the mantel was acquired at the estate sale and then given to the Society by the purchaser. At present the furniture in this room is on loan to the Society.

Dining Room—The walls were painted a soft yellow and the floors varnished. The Society took a reproduction portrait of Sarah Bullock and placed it in an antique frame which makes an attractive memento in its position over the mantel. Soon this room will be emptied of the present furniture and assistance in replacing it is urgently needed. At the windows of the dining room (as well as in the living room and library) are panels of lace fabric typical of the era.

The kitchen and rest rooms are to be the next projects. For the house to be used this is a necessary improvement. This work can only begin when funds are available.

The second floor which consists of five bedrooms is a real challenge since there will have to be more cleaning done. Two rooms have been assigned to special projects. One will be a children's museum planned and used by Barbara Dean. About $880.00 was given for the Cora

Room in memory of Bea Brown, Barbara's mother. Work on this room has already begun involving electrical wiring, carpentry, etc. If any readers own an antique toy or book, please consider donating it—perhaps in memory of someone. Another bedroom is to be a railroad museum planned and carried out by Billy Steele. The needed wiring is already being placed. A third bedroom is planned to be refurbished as a typical bedroom of that era and, as might be expected, appropriate donations will be appreciated. The remaining bedrooms and attic will also constitute challenges for clearing and cleaning.

The surrounding grounds require a tremendous amount of work for landscaping in keeping with the house and the times. The garage has been closed and painted in a manner complementary to the house and to provide storage space. The space between the house is to be used for parking. This is not exactly in keeping with the nineteenth century, but there is really no choice if 20 to 30 cars are to be provided for.

The Society has had tremendous support from the members as well as from the City of Eastman and Dodge County.

Iron railings have been added to both sides of the front steps and a wheel chair access provided to the side porch.

Expenses must be met to include insurance, electric power, cleaning, yard improvement and maintenance, heating and even postage. Toward this end we have 114 paid memberships representing 191 people.

These newsletters are issued eleven times a year and the present officers of the Society were elected in January for a two-year term.

February 1996

THE J. C. ROGERS—R. C. LEWIS HOUSE
800 SIXTH AVENUE, EASTMAN

When a house is focused on from a historical point of view, the structure quite often becomes of secondary importance to the past occupants. The home on 800 Sixth Avenue was known as the W. C. Edwards house a few years ago; however, it is now known as the R. C. Lewis house.

The home was built in 1899 by Sheriff James Cullen (J. C.) Rogers in a section of town called Dodge Park. It was a special part of town wherein the houses in general were built and inhabited by doctors, lawyers, and county officials. Most of the men walked to work which probably created a great camaraderie. The houses in Dodge Park were similar in appearance and design.

The house at 800 Sixth Avenue was built as a rather simple six-room house in 1899 with a square central hall and rear additions. There is a double front door with side windows and transom panels. The front porch wraps around both sides with Tuscan columns. Five gables make up the roof with the first gable housing an extremely intricate shingling pattern; the back gables have only the saw tooth pattern of shingling.

The first owner of this house was J. C. Rogers. He was born April 27, 1860. He was Dodge County sheriff with his first term at the age of 32 beginning in 1893 and continuing to 1896; his second term was from 1897 to 1900; third term from 1905 to 1907 whereupon he died in office at the age of 44. He was sheriff of the County through a crucial time. The two-story Victorian style jail was built in 1897 and a new courthouse was built in 1906. The over-riding problem which plagued Sheriff Rogers during all of his years in office was the Dodge land litigations. He had to continually assist U.S. marshals in locating defendants and witnesses. Sheriff Rogers was the grandson of Thomas Rogers, one of the four Rogers brothers who were pioneer settlers here long before the creation of Dodge County. It is interesting to note that Grover Cleveland Rogers (G. C.), who was also a Dodge County sheriff, was a half-brother to J. C. Rogers. A number of years later Ollie B. Peacock was elected sheriff and he was a second cousin of J. C. Rogers.

At the death of J. C. Rogers, his wife, Lucy Rogers, inherited the home place.

The third owner of this house was R. T. Jackson who inherited it from Lucy Rogers, his niece. Mrs. R. T. Jackson (Eloise) was the fourth owner of the property and she sold the house to her mother-in-law, Mrs. Lou Dora Jackson.

The sixth owner of the house was Burlie Jackson Edwards, the daughter of Lou Dora Jackson and the wife of W. C. Edwards. About the turn of the century, as young boys, W.C. and his brother, Lewis, had ridden bicycles for three days from Lake Butler, Florida to Eastman, Georgia. Walter Carr chose to work for Milton Edwards, his uncle, in the mercantile business and he later began a furniture store. Burlie and W. C. Sr. were valued citizens of the County. At the death of Burlie Jackson Edwards and W. C., Sr., the furniture store was willed to W. C., Jr. He was successful in creating an outstanding furniture store in the town as well as serving in many capacities for the advancement of the community. His sister, Dorothy Edwards Aldridge, inherited the home place in 1961.

The past owners of the house had had a family relationship from Sheriff Rogers to this stage. R. C. Lewis bought the property from Aldridge with intentions of restoring it. Billy and Nancy Steele had set their minds and hearts on the same project and prevailed on R. C. to let them have the house. They moved in with anticipation of restoring this old home to its original beauty. They worked on the house for about two years before moving to their own homestead, the Steele home place on Cochran Road.

The last and present owner of this historic house is R. C. Lewis. Mr. Lewis is a retired master carpenter and has used his talent in creating a showplace of it. The entire inside of the house with an added second floor, the outside with its freshly painted look and beautified landscaping of the grounds all combine to create a beautiful place.

This is one of the original houses in Dodge Park and the City of Eastman.

July 1995

SINGLE AND DOUBLE PEN LOG HOUSES IN DODGE COUNTY

A goodly number of log houses built in Dodge County prior to the Civil War were still standing as late as 1940. Three log homes, which continued to be occupied throughout the first half of the present century, were located about four miles south of Eastman. These houses, two of which eventually had several rooms, all began as single pen log homes constructed after the land between the Oconee and the Ocmulgee Rivers was opened to settlement following the Indian removal in 1804.

The A. J. Hargrove home was located just north of what is known today as Hargrove Crossing. Andrew Jackson Hargrove, the builder of this house, and his wife Nancy Hendley Hargrove were the parents of eleven children who were reared there. The picture of Mrs. Hargrove and her son Larkin (Lark) which appears in Mrs. W. P. Cobb's *History of Dodge County* was made in the yard of this log home. While living with his mother and father, Lark left Dodge County to serve in the Civil War. The Hargrove house began as one log pen. Later two additional pens were added across an open hall, creating what was referred to as a "dogtrot." This house was dismantled in the 1960s and moved to the home of Audrey Hargrove

Cofield near Rhine. A line of mobile homes now occupies the site in the pecan orchard where the Hargrove home once stood.

Jordan Brown, the first sheriff of Dodge County, built a home south of Hargrove Crossing. This log house had to be moved about thirty yards when the Macon and Brunswick Railroad, a railroad Jordan Brown helped to construct, was built through Dodge County in 1869 to 1870. Jordan Brown married Jane Hargrove, the daughter of Andrew Jackson Hargrove and Nancy Hendley Hargrove. Jordan Brown and Jane Hargrove Brown were the parents of four children, Mollie, Morgan, Fannie, and Charles. Mr. Charlie Brown inherited the place from his father and before the log portion was removed in the 1940s reared five children there: Harry Brown, Jordan Brown, Gladys Brown Graham, Louise Brown Driggers, and Ruby Lee Brown Shadburn. The additions to this log house were incorporated into another house, which stands today.

Ovid Vickers, August 1996

THE UPLANDS HOTEL

Completed in 1876, the Uplands Hotel would have inspired the pride of any southern community, but its construction among the pines, where large buildings were rare, made it even more imposing. Three stories high, with a mansard roof, widow's walk, and tall brick chimneys, the structure loomed high above a lawn planted in trees and shrubs and enclosed by a white picket fence. The Uplands one hundred rooms, elegant parlors, dining rooms, and billiard room were comfortably furnished and its airy veranda was lined with Boston rockers. The dining room was unsurpassed in its arrangement and supply of linens. Staffed by managers, cashiers and chefs from Adirondack resort hotels and New York City restaurants, the Uplands was a favorite stopping place for northerners on their trips through the Deep South. It is recorded in the local newspapers that during the first week in April 1881, nine out of ten guests were Yankees, almost all from Massachusetts and New York. The place also became a haven of sorts for Northerners desperate for cures for respiratory diseases.

Part of the magic that transformed upstart Eastman from an insignificant railroad depot to a thriving town of six to seven hundred was the tourist industry. The Macon and Brunswick Railroad had hardly been completed when Eastman began to gain a reputation as a stopping point for Yankee tourists bound for sunny Florida.

The Eastman Hotel Company was incorporated in 1873 with an initial capital of $10,000.00 and the privilege of increasing the capitalization to $25,000.00. Mr. Eastman donated about six acres for the hotel establishment stipulating that the Company would at no time sell or use the property for anything but hotel business and that the land not covered by the building be kept as ornamental grounds with paths and drives. The Corporation met and elected five trustees as follows: Messrs. A. G. P. Dodge, N. W. Dodge, W. P. Eastman, James Bishop and Henry Neimann. The elected officers were: W. P. Eastman, President; Mr. A. G. Dodge, Treasurer; and Mr. W. F. Moss, Secretary.

The hotel was placed on the area situated between Seventh Avenue on the north, Fifth Avenue on the south, with Main Street (alongside the railway) on the east and Eastman Way on the west. It was suitable to be on Main Street since the patrons arrived by railway, in fact many had their own private rail cars. The passengers would disembark and walk on the covered walkway from the Station to the Hotel.

The first manager of the Uplands was C. N. Scofield and his equally accomplished wife, Mrs. Scofield. Their son, Fred, worked in the office and under the management of this team the hotel was a success, financially and otherwise. The Scofields managed in the summer the Windsor Hotel in the Adironback area of New York, and on their return to Eastman the next winter they were welcomed back by the many friends they had gained the previous season.

The hotel was named Uplands in recognition of William E. Dodge's description of the territory on the sole visit he made to Dodge County. In the speech he made dedicating the new courthouse, he said that the terrain of the area was neither hilly nor was it flat, it was just upland; thus, the name was later applied to the new hotel. The hotel was open during the winter season, opening in January and closing May 1.

The second known manager of the hotel was Mr. B. Lindsay as announced in the *Eastman Times*: "Messrs. Lindsay and Sons are the most popular landlords in the United States. Their admirers visit them by thousands at their house in the White Mountains in the summer and follow them to their house among the Pines in the winter."

Idolene Fitzgerald Montgomery, the daughter of Julia Peacock Fitzgerald, recalled the many stories her mother used to tell about the excitement at the Uplands Hotel. Ashburn Street—later renamed Seventh Avenue—separated the Peacock family home (Ms. Fitzgerald's parents) and the Uplands Hotel. Grand entertainment was planned for the guests with bands being imported from New York and staying a week at a time. Other types of entertainment were also available such as bowling, badminton, croquet and horseback riding.

The community also used the beautiful and spacious facilities. In the *History of Dodge County* by Mrs. W. P. Cobb, there is mention about the organization and meetings of the W. C. T. U. in 1904. "The first social meeting of the Union, held at the Uplands Hotel in the winter of 1904, was a pronounced success. Every family in the Town of Eastman received a written invitation to this affair."

By the early 1880s the Uplands Hotel had become a winter resort for northern capitalists. Southerners realized the Yankees had the capital they needed to put the region back on its feet and the Uplands Hotel became the place where northern money and southern commercial ambitions were joined. The process of greater unity between the North and the South was hastened by social gatherings and joint business ventures, not to mention the generous donations of northern visitors to the local community. New Yorkers visiting the Uplands in 1881, for instance, donated carpeting and Sunday School books to an Eastman church.

The Uplands Hotel was one of the first luxury hotels in the south expressly for tourists. It flourished for nearly thirty years before burning in 1907.

February 1995

Comment: Some years after the Uplands Hotel burned, the Lee-Land Hotel was built on the same plot of land. This hotel existed until the early 1960s, when it was torn down. The Citizens Bank now stands on the former location of both hotels. Pictures of both hotels are included in the photograph section of this book.

HISTORIC EASTMAN BUS STATION RECEIVES NATIONAL RECOGNITION

Dr. W. Ray Luce, Division Director and Deputy State Historic Preservation Officer, Georgia Department of National Resources, has announced the listing of the former Eastman Bus Station in the National Register of Historic Places effective May 30, 2002. Owned by the City of Eastman, the Eastman Bus Station at 305 College Street was built from 1945 to 1946 by John T. Wilbanks as a bus station and telegraph office with the owner/manager's residence on the second floor. It was listed in the National Register at the state level of significance for its architecture and historic transportation associations as a rare surviving example of a historic bus station in Georgia. It is one of only three known recorded historic bus stations in the state and the only one which includes a residence. Robin B. Nail, Historic Preservation Planner with the Heart of Georgia Altamaha Regional Development Center (RDC), prepared the National Register nomination.

The National Register of Historic Places is the federal government's list of properties determined worthy of preservation. National Register properties are recognized for their significance at the national, state, or local level, with most listed for their local historical significance. The Eastman Bus Station joins three other Dodge County properties in the National Register. They are: the Dodge County Courthouse; the Eastman House, and the Williamson Mausoleum at Orphan's Cemetery. There are presently a total of 51 National Register-listed properties in the 17-county Heart of Georgia Altamaha RDC Region, including 3 historic districts and 48 individual properties. The City of Eastman purchased the Eastman Bus Station in 1999. The station continued to operate as a bus station until 1983 and later housed a florist business. The building is currently [2002] undergoing a phased rehabilitation for multi-purpose community use. The Heart of Georgia Altamaha RDC has assisted the City with obtaining two Georgia Heritage Grants for the rehabilitation project.

DODGE COUNTY COURT HOUSES

Dodge County was created by an Act of the General Assembly on October 26, 1870. The creation of the county was planned by Mr. William Pitt Eastman. The town named after him was purposely placed in the center of the proposed county in order for Eastman to become the county seat. At that time Mr. Eastman told his friend, Mr. William E. Dodge, that if he would build the county a courthouse, he would name the county for him. Mr. Dodge expressed his appreciation of the honor conferred upon him by building at his own expense what was then a magnificent courthouse and presented it to the citizens of the county. It was erected where the present courthouse now stands and was a two story frame structure which cost about $25,000 [equivalent to $500,000 in 2019 dollars]. The courthouse was completed in 1874.

In 1908 the first courthouse was torn down for the erection of a more spacious facility with an impressive edifice designed by architect E. C. Hosford, an Eastman native. As Mrs. Cobb said in her *History of Dodge County*: "It is a most attractive work of architecture, contains all conveniences, and was completed in 1908 at a cost of $125,000." This handsome building was enjoyed until May 4, 1939.

Orene Mullis Burns related many memories of the building since her father, C. N. Mullis, was sheriff from 1914 to 1929 and the family lived in the sheriff quarters. She recalled Mr. Emory Reid coming to the courthouse every week to set the clock which was in the dome. The town folks depended on the courthouse clock. She also remembers that the jurors spent the night while deliberating in the north-east corner of the top floor during the trials; the offices were much larger than those of today and interestingly a Dr. Burch had an office in the basement.

Unfortunately, fire broke out during the night of May 4, 1939 in the center of the building and the dome quickly collapsed. County Commissioner, W. D. McCranie, said the damage to the building was covered by insurance in the amount of $39,000 and that insurance of $6,000 was carried on the furniture and $1,000 on the records. Fortunately, there was only slight damage to the county's permanent records.

The county immediately started the rebuilding of another courthouse. The price of construction was much higher than it was for the previous building and the total insurance collected did not cover the cost. This necessitated careful planning. The courthouse of today was built on the same foundation but minus the dome and entrances on each side of the building. The building today is practical but without the elegance of the dome, the varied roof line, impressive balconies and columns. The County has had three fine courthouses and there is pride in the history of the structures.

FOLLOWING ARE EXCERPTS FROM THE *GEORGIA BENCH AND BAR, VOL. 1* BY WARREN GRICE

The Oconee Circuit of Georgia's Judicial System was created by the Act approved December 12, 1871, and included Dodge and surrounding counties. The *Hawkinsville Dispatch*, in its issue of May 2, 1872 reported an early sitting of the court in the new circuit. "At noon, on Thursday, the Judge, Honorable A. C. Pate, (the Circuit's first judge) and the Bar, proceeded on the cars to Station No. 11, Macon & Brunswick Railroad, just twenty miles below Eastman (apparently McRae). Arriving at the site, "Sheriff Hatton conducted the court a couple of hundred yards in the midst of a thick grove of pine saplings." Reference is made to the fact that the court was "deprived of the comfortable accommodations of a superbly arranged edifice, erected by the lavish hand of wealth, such an one as we had left an hour before (the first courthouse of the new County of Dodge, the gift of

William E. Dodge, of New York) yet the new seat of justice was not void of attractions or destitute of comforts."

The early history of the Oconee Circuit tells in great detail of the events of Sunday, August 6, 1882, when a riot resulted in the death of a young man who was "beaten into insensibility and then shot and beaten to death with pickets snatched from the fence by members of the blood-thirsty mob." A number of the perpetrators were tried before Judge Pate, and convicted. Five of them were "dropped to their death at the same moment on October 20, 1882, in the courthouse yard—perhaps the largest number of people ever legally executed at the same time in any place in the United States."

Judge Pate, when his temper was aroused, would "not be choice in his language to those who vexed him, but would afterward apologize for his rudeness." Once he used some violent language toward a prominent member of the bar. The sitting Judge fined him for contempt, and "to his dying day, he kept in his pocketbook this receipt which he was very fond of showing: " 'Rec'd of Anthony C. Pate ten dollars in full of a fine imposed by D. M. Roberts, Judge Superior Court, for calling (name not given) in open court a (*expletive #*@&^%)* liar.' "

Early records show that the Dodge Bar included D. M. Roberts, John F. DeLacy, James Bishop, Jr. (a former resident of the Eastman House), E. A. Smith, J. E. Wooten, B. S. Milner, B. R. Calhoun, Walter M. Clements, and Elias Herrman.

No history of the Oconee Circuit would be complete without mentioning names of several of our past and present Historical Society members. Julia Smith was among the earlier women admitted to the Georgia Bar. (She was one of three lawyers admitted at one time, the others being Herman Talmadge and Carter Peterson). We can also boast of having as members two former Presidents of the State Bar of Georgia, Will Ed Smith and Wilton D. Harrington.

July 1997

TOWNS AND COMMUNITIES OF DODGE COUNTY

HISTORY OF CHESTER, GEORGIA

The little town of Chester lies in the northern corner of Dodge, a diamond-shaped county in the center of Georgia. This geographical setting has served to somewhat isolate the community from the rest of the county. Often it has been more convenient for citizens of Chester to travel and do their shopping in Laurens and Bleckley counties. Separated from Eastman, the county seat, by fifteen miles of forests, fields, and Gum Swamp Creek, Chester arose, flourished and declined, and grew again in relative isolation.

No one seems to know where the name "Chester" originated. The subject of much conjecture, there are many theories but little hard evidence. On the other hand, a famous road just north of town got its name from the Native Americans that populated the area before the white man arrived. The very first maps of the Chester Territory, drawn before the town itself was founded, show a trail labeled "Chickasaw Path". The name later mutated into "Chicken Road" when settlers arrived.

Chester, the northernmost town in Dodge County began as a peach orchard in the early 1900s. The Orchard, and later the town, was situated on two gently sloping hills with a small stream, a tributary of Gum Swamp, in the middle. As disease began to decimate the peach trees, the manager, T. C. Byrd, was given orders by the owner to break the orchard up into lots to sell. A brass band was hired to play for the occasion, and barbeque was served during the big land sale.

Citizens who were formerly employed by the orchard found employment in the lumber and turpentine industry, which flourished in the area. For many years afterward, up into the 1970s one could stumble upon huge sawdust piles in the middle of the woods surrounding Chester, remnants of those days gone by. Mr. June Williams ran this industry, which largely met its demise when the main turpentine still burned in 1900.

The first buildings in Chester arose on Highway 257, which ran from Dublin, through Chester, Roddy, Yonkers, Empire and on to Hawkinsville and Albany.

A cafeteria was run by an Aunt Lou Beach. Chester's first mayor was W. B. Jessup and the postmaster, unusual for that time, was an African-American named John Hall.

Chester's first train was built to haul lumber and gum from the sawmills and turpentine stills. Later the tracks were re-aligned and the Wrightsville-Tennille Railroad was established. This was an important development in the town, for its citizens could now travel to Dublin to shop. This was an early example of how Chester people relied more on Laurens County than on Dodge—there was no regular transportation there and back. Some of Chester's students rode the train to school each day.

Chester's town charter was granted by the State in 1902 and the community grew rapidly. The town was incorporated as a City on August 21, 1916, with Mayor John T. Currie presiding. The first water system was developed by R. L. Jackson, later to be sold to W. P. McClelland. Windmills pumped the water then but were replaced much later by electric motors.

Lonnie Smith, who ran a movie theater, put up Chester's first lights—he strung "them all over town" according to local historians. In 1936 Georgia Power entered the scene.

Chester Banking Company began in 1909, with D. A. Burch as president. When this bank closed, W. S. Wynn and C. M. Rogers opened a private bank. Today Chester's bank is a branch of the Bank of Dodge County. A story is told by Chester's longtime mailman, Billy McLeod, of a Chester farmer who traveled to Eastman in 1929 to sell his harvest of cotton. After receiving his profits, he walked over to the bank to deposit the cash. However, the shades were drawn on the door and a teller was busy locking up. The bank was not supposed to close for several more minutes, so the farmer begged her to let him deposit his money, otherwise, he would have to go home to Chester and ride back to Eastman by horse the next day. But no amount of talking could convince the teller to let him in. 'We are closed", she said firmly. Mad as a hornet, the farmer went home that evening, planning to return the next day to give the Bank president and that teller a piece of his mind.

When he returned the next morning, however, he was in for a shock. The bank had failed. Whoever had money in the banks lost everything, for the stock market crash of 1929 had hit. That obnoxious teller had saved him his fortune.

In another story often told by people around Chester, the school building was blown off its foundation in 1929. The school trustees had to borrow $15,000 to repair the school. The check came in on the four o'clock train, but the bank did not open the next morning because of the crash. All their deposited money was lost! The trustees had to borrow an additional $15,000 to fix the building.

During its heyday, many businesses thrived in Chester. A list of some of the best known would include C. M.

Rogers and Son, W. S. Wynn, J. M. Bryant, Betty Jessup's hat shop, Herman Floyd's telephone company, and moving up to modern times, Cannon's Drugs, Ronnie Sawyer's Food Mart, Paul's Café, Hon's Automotive, and Brown's Auto Parts.

Many children who grew up in Chester can remember going to Johnny Dykes' store for an ice cream cone, and riding out to Malone's Lake to swim and be nibbled by fish.

Chester had four doctors over the years who made a lasting impact. G. W. Bordeaux made his rounds in a horse and buggy. Dr. W. F. Massey, who began as a teacher, wrote of making his house calls on a motorcycle. Dr. Massey had a drug store in his office.

Dr. Pablo Agahan is something of an enigma and a mystery. Coming to Chester in the 1970s he ended up giving free medical care for many folks, but he is best remembered for his meticulously researched history of the town. Dr. Agahan disappeared and was never seen again, even when his possessions were sold off in a big sale.

As in many southern towns, for awhile cotton was king in Chester, which boasted two cotton gins. One big cotton gin burned down in the middle of the night during the 1960s. It was a sight many Chester citizens will never forget. The fire silenced the constant hum of the gin, which permeates the memories of many to this day.

Math Parkerson was a barber in Chester for about sixty years. Thousands of fish stories were repeated in his old shop. Mr. Parkerson's name is immortalized in huge letters on the city's old water tank, and it has been that way for decades. When questioned about it Mr. Math revealed that a friend of his did it one night while inebriated.

Chester's first school was outside of town and the Rev. J. R. Harvey was the first teacher. Later the large brick building downtown was used until Chester's main school building was erected in 1927. These times brought in the era of school busses and lunchrooms. The people of Chester were always involved with their school, even building the Chester gymnasium using local lumber. Many exciting games and shows were held in that old gym over the years. In the 1970s the Lion's Club "Battle of Guitars" drew huge crowds to the otherwise small town.

Mayor Doug Rogers brought sweeping changes to the community when he took office in the 1980s. Rogers was responsible for landing a major employment opportunity for Chester: Dodge Correctional Institution. He also modernized the town with a new water and sewage disposal system complete with a state of the art sewage pond.

Now, in the mid-1990s Chester faces the problems of many small towns. Metropolitan areas attract many of the town's young people, who often never return to their roots, and in a sense, their history is lost. But on the other hand, tiny communities like Chester can offer what no big city can: safe streets, family atmosphere, and people who know and care for each other. The people of Chester wouldn't have it any other way.

Donnie Screws, October 1994

RHINE, DODGE COUNTY, GEORGIA

In 1889, this "backwoods" settlement was well established on a "ridge" running eastward from the east side of the Ocmulgee River, six miles toward the rising sun and four miles east of the once prosperous river town of Copeland, Georgia. With the decline of the riverboat passenger service and the surveying and grading underway for the new extension of the Savannah, Americus, and Montgomery Railway from Abbeville east to Lyons, many Copeland families and businesses were on the move down the right-of-way to the new settlement.

A settler, James M. Swymer, had obtained this desirable, well drained ridge with its good timber, streams and spring from the Dodge Land and Lumber Company. It was part of the Fourteenth Land District of the newly established Dodge County. This ridge was to become the basis for the development of the town of Rhine, named for the German river.

A charter was granted by the General Assembly for the town of Rhine. Its limits were not to exceed one-half mile in any of the four directions from Jim Swymer's Store. This charter became official September 1, 1891. Elections were then held in December for Rhine's new officers. Churches sprung up along with schools. A brick jail was constructed and a town marshal was hired. A grist and flour mill was constructed along Henley Creek. Rhine had a public water system consisting of a hand operated iron pitcher pump in a well in the center of town.

The Robitszch brothers constructed a building on what was becoming the main street; the Ryals brothers, D. W. and G. W., built their large general store. Jim Reaves, the Maloys and still another German, John Womble, bought land from Swymer to build their houses and businesses. Other families converging on the "ridge" were the Coffees, Mizells, Martins, Yanceys, Studstills, McCranies, Bryans, Harrells, Browns, Clements, and many more. The area was becoming an agricultural and turpentine center. In 1889 the Post Office was officially closed in Copeland and moved to Rhine. Passenger and freight trains arrived and departed from Rhine. The most famous of them was the "Shoo-Fly."

Jim Swymer gave land for the first school on the east side of town; later, the building burned and was replaced with a two-story structure containing an auditorium on the top level. Rhine Baptist Church was organized in 1891 and St. James Baptist Church was one of the oldest churches in Rhine having been established by Jim Tony Maloy and his mother, Becky Maloy. The white congregation of old Allston Methodist Episcopal church

South moved to Rhine leaving Allston (Austin) to the black congregation.

Rhine's first cemetery was at the rear of Bay Springs Methodist Church and later it became a community cemetery. The Maloy mansion was built across from Dr. W. C. Maloy's office.

The Griffin Mizell family moved to Rhine and built the first hotel, a two-story building near the depot. Rhine had four doctors during those early years: Dr. W. C. Maloy, Dr. Sonny Williamson, Dr. Coffee, Dr. Burch and a dentist, Dr. Jones. There were board sidewalks, hitching posts and oil-lantern street lamps along the main streets and business section. Rhine tried to keep a town marshal but failed. The City Aldermen kept this ad in the local county newspaper: "Wanted, Marshal, salary and guaranteed funeral expenses."

R. E. Ponder came to Rhine in 1903 and later established a turpentine business and other enterprises.

Rhine school burned one night during a picture show. A fifteen thousand dollar bond issue was floated to enable rebuilding. The school was replaced with a brick building. Georgia Power Company turned on the power in Rhine in 1934. Windmills were shut down when electric pumps were installed in wells.

In 1936 the school gymnasium was completed at no cost to the Dodge County Board of Education or taxpayers. In 1936 the Rhine boys' basketball team went to the State Tournament and won the State Championship trophy. In 1938 T. K. Carroll came to Rhine as the first agricultural instructor and led the effort in getting a canning plant and potato cutting house for community use.

War was declared in 1941 and a Draft Board was set up and many young Rhine men were drafted. The first World War II casualty was Seaman First Class Theron McCranie and others included Freddie Pelter Day (USMC), Thurmon Harrell, Maloy Conley, and Verna Lee Higgins.

In the late 1940s Rhine was first in Dodge County to install a traffic light. In the 1950s the first television sets came to Rhine with a seventy-five foot antenna for each set. In 1953 the twelfth grade was added as a requirement for graduation. The Rhine Community House and the new City Hall, including a jail and a one-bay fire station, were built.

In 1972 an Early Childhood Program was added to the Rhine School curriculum. More streets were paved and guttered. Rhine Elementary School moved to consolidated schools located in Eastman at the beginning of the 1990-91 school year.

The special event for 1991 was the sixteenth Pondtown Festival and Rhine Centennial Celebration.

JAYBIRD SPRINGS : LOCAL RESORT AREA

Jaybird Springs is associated with pleasant activities by the young and the old of Central Georgia. The public perception of the place has varied from wide and favorable knowledge to near oblivion in recent years but it has begun a comeback beginning in the 1980s under the guidance of new owners, Denise and Terry Katz.

Jaybird is approximately 14 miles south of Eastman and three miles to the east of U.S. Highway 341 on Jaybird Road. The land which T. A. McMillan purchased to develop the Springs area was set up originally as a 40-acre tract. He drilled a deep well to provide water under pressure for the fountain head. There are 24 different minerals in the water and it is reputed to hold healing powers for skin diseases and kidney ailments.

Visitors came from all over Georgia and surrounding states in search of health. Many came for a pleasant vacation either camping or relaxing for an extended time in the grand hotel. The limousine which customarily met the visitors was an open air 1906 touring sedan. It picked them up at the Helena Railroad Depot. Entertainment was planned, orchestra music was provided and the general atmosphere was outstanding. The swimming pool was the largest in the state when it was built in 1906 and these waters too were said to have great curative powers. What most visitors seem to remember is that the water was the coldest to be found anywhere.

Carrie Walker, daughter of T. A. McMillan, says that the 1930s decade was especially exciting because of various statewide Gospel Singing Conventions held on the last Sunday in May and the first Sunday in September each year. Tremendous crowds came from all over Georgia and neighboring states for these events. The largest crowd recorded totaled about 10,000 who were attracted by the word that Eugene Talmadge would speak at one of the Sings.

In 1938 T. A. Bland purchased Jaybird Springs and initiated a prosperous era with somewhat different emphasis than previously. Bland sold 5-gallon bottles of water in all of the surrounding counties. It was bottled, loaded and delivered by truck directly to the buyers' homes. During this period many young couples and families were drawn to the resort for entertainment. The hotel had previously been destroyed by fire, hence the social activities were of a more casual nature than earlier. During the next several decades the fun activities were skating, miniature golf, swimming, and bowling. During this period T. A. Bland sold the property to his daughter,

Edith, and her husband, Alto Deese. The couple provided additional energy to the resort management and under their good business sense and firm guidance the Springs continued to prosper. There were many family reunions every weekend using the picnic shelters. The popularity of the location for these reunions also led to a sense of safety and security for the young people involved.

The Deeses sold the property in 1983 to Mike Hufstetler. During the next ten or fifteen years there was a reduction in emphasis on family gatherings and public entertainment places. The Hufstetlers sold to Bill Clark who emphasized the restaurant part of the resort. Jaybird Springs was becoming an attraction of the past and those who had enjoyable experiences in the past began to be saddened at this outcome.

In 1994 a young couple, Denise and Terry Katz, committed themselves to the acquisition with a view toward reversing the decline. They are hardworking and determined to restore the past glory of the resort. A large softball park has been completed and fenced, the usual attractions have been repaired and updated, and there is presently a pervasive sense of activity and excitement. They are working hard and becoming increasingly affiliated as well with the surrounding towns. These efforts are exciting confidence and producing good will. They report of as many as six family reunions a week along with a steady flow of young people. Churches are using the grounds for special occasions and some have held evening services under the shelters.

Jaybird Springs is still a favorite playground in this region.

August 1995

GREAT EXCITEMENT AT CHAUNCEY

Mullingar is a village about one-half mile from Chauncey, named in honor of its proprietor, Mr. James Mullin. It is the site of a wooden roof shingle manufacturing plant owned by Mr. Mullin.

Mr. Mullin is one of our enterprising citizens who keep up with the rapid progress of the age. Recently he conceived the idea that he might greatly facilitate his business and economize time and labor by use of one of the much talked of telephones, which would put him in easy speaking distance to his station. The idea was no sooner conceived than carried into effect. He at once made his order and the telephone arrived in Chauncey at the train station last Saturday night.

Monday morning (we will not mention the Sunday part of it) he went to work putting up poles, very much on the order of telegraph poles. Very soon the poles were up, the small metal wire stretched and fastened, reaching from his office to the store house—a distance of nearly one-half mile. Mr. M says he wanted to make as little ado about it as possible for really he had very little confidence in it after he saw it. But now everything ready, the thing must be tested. So Mr. Mullin in his office at one end of the line and Dr. J.W. Tucker in the store at the other end proceeded.

> Tucker: Hello!
> Mullin: Yes
> Tucker: How's this?
> Mullin: Bully! Just the thing? Grand!

And thus they continued to converse to their hearts' content in an ordinary tone of voice.

Hearing of this new enterprise in our perambulations on Tuesday, we availed ourselves of an opportunity yesterday to visit it. We went directly to Mr. Mullin's and were soon in conversation with parties at the station. The whole thing is certainly very simple and cheap. This one cost only $8.17. Mr. Mullin is decidedly pleased with it and proposes to put one from his commissary to his office. It is certainly a decided success and we congratulate Mr. Mullin upon his taking the lead in this enterprise.

Extracted from the Eastman Times, March 1878

Comments: Mullingar section of Chauncey named for Mr. Mullin.

A LETTER TO THE EDITOR
EASTMAN TIMES, MAR. 28, 1878

Mr. Editor:

Down at Chauncey the other day I was sitting in the store of Mr. W. K. Bussey, chatting lazily when a faint shrill "Heigh—lo" startled us. I thought it came from the other store or from somewhere else a hundred yards away. Mr. Bussey thought differently. "Ough", said he, bouncing to his feet, "did you hear that?" And going to one corner of the store room he jumped upon a goods box, stuck his mouth on an oyster-can-looking thing fixed to the wall, and sang out "Hey! Who's there?"

And then a still, small voice was heard speaking in tones so soft and weird that to me, as I sat some distance away, seemed to come from the spirit world.

Mr. Bussey asked if I wished to talk through the telephone. Of course I did. He introduced me to Mr. Mullin whose office was at the other end of the line, half a mile away, and stepping up to the instrument I asked him a question. Back came the answer in words so natural and distinct that for the life of me I could not help laughing. Did you ever converse through a small aperture in a thick solid wall? The word and tone there, I think, would very well represent those through the telephone. The words were as distinct as if we had been in adjoining rooms with the door between us about an inch ajar. The slightest emphasis with every characteristic of the voice is readily distinguished. At another time in the day a young man in the office of Mr. Mullin sang us two songs, every word and note of which were distinct to all who were standing near. This telephone is a decided success and I sent my congratulations to Mr. Mullin over the wire.

I hear that a gentleman in Chauncey speaks of establishing telephone communication between his house and the church. That might be a good rainy day idea but suppose everybody should adopt the plan. It might be fun to those seated cozily at home but it would be death to the ardor of the preacher. Think of his hurling the thunders and his eloquence at rows of oyster cans ranged along the wall.

From the Eastman Times

A JOURNEY TWENTY MILES THROUGH PINES AND WIREGRASS (*EASTMAN TIMES* 1879)

We returned from Eastman to Hawkinsville last week by private conveyance–traveling the old and direct road. The distance is twenty miles, which we made with a pair of horses in about three hours. Our companion was Mr. Henry Waterman.

The country between Eastman and Hawkinsville is rolling and exceedingly pretty, with an immense growth of the finest yellow pine timber, and a perpetual growth of wiregrass, O, that wonder to many people! Upon this grass, cattle and sheep subsist during the entire year. In the spring and summer they become perfectly sleek, and the beef and mutton, when thoroughly fat, are equal to that of any other country. It is not an unusual thing at this season of the year to find a man who pens daily from forty to one hundred cows with spring calves. There is a bountiful supply of milk and butter for three months in the year, when, in July or August, the cows and calves are all turned out together and driven into the woods to gather fat and strength to carry them through the winter. The season for milk and butter is then over and you can scarcely get a glass of milk or butter enough for a biscuit in a whole day's travel. Occasionally a man will keep a couple of cows and pasture them upon his fields after the crops have been harvested.

We do not often travel through a prettier section of country than that between Eastman and Hawkinsville, and yet there are probably not more than eight or a dozen families living on the whole route—twenty miles. The country would maintain a large population. The lands are rolling and are well drained. The soil is thin but is easily cultivated and yields generously with a little help. The little pimples upon the surface indicated a good foundation, and attest the durability of the land, and its adaptability to the growth of cotton, corn, oats, sweet potatoes, sugar cane and other southern products.

The country is very healthy, and the genial climate, the cheapness of the land, the abundance of wood, the advantages of a limitless range for cattle, render it a most desirable section for people seeking homes. Mr. Waterman told us that not long ago he was traveling through this section in company with Mr. Holeman, a western stock drover, when the latter stated that the country reminded him more of California than any country he had ever visited.

On the route we passed the old Harrell homestead—the place where the Harrell brothers were raised—the boyhood home of William, Lovett, Levi, Wright, and John Harrell, all of whom are living in Pulaski and Dodge counties within less than twenty miles of the familiar spot. The property is now owned, we believe, by George H. Hazlehurst of Macon, former President of the M & B. R. R. [Macon and Brunswick RR]. The land has been in cultivation for many years and instead of being worn out and washed away, appears as good as ever. The place is in charge of the tenant.

As we came by the plantation of our old friend, Alex Reagan, we were glad to observe many evidences of thrift and prosperity. We noticed patches of fine corn, cane, and potatoes, and considerable fresh ground cleared timber, timber deadened, new fencing, etc.

There should be fifty more pretty farms and neat dwellings on the route. There is plenty of room and nobody would be crowded. They would aid in keeping up schools in their respective neighborhoods, building churches, lessening county taxation and be advantageous to the country in many other ways.

We hope there may be a speedy demand for the lands by immigrants from other sections, and that the encroachments of the turpentine hunters may cease. The turpentine farms are injuring the country. The timber is being destroyed rapidly and the destruction of the timber will render the lands almost valueless.

What we want to see along this route is a picture of happy farm life—thrifty little farms, neat dwellings, orchards, etc. We would like to see each farmer's house surrounded with rosebushes, flowers, fruit trees, small groves in front, little vineyards, etc., all of which would cost but a small sum compared with their value and comfort. These evidences of taste would be inviting to strangers, and would enhance the value of every man's home.

March 1994

PLACE NAMES IN DODGE COUNTY

The history of Dodge County is reflected in the names of the county's towns, villages, and crossroads. Although many place names are associated with families living in the area before the creation of the county, the major population centers, including the city of Eastman, were named for persons who came into the county during the late 1800's when timber was the major industry.

It is also interesting that although the Creek Indians were living in this area of Georgia when the first settlers arrived, only three names in the county are of the Indian origin, and they relate to the word "ocmulgee." The Creek word "ocmulgee" most probably means "gathering place" since *–ulgee* is a standard Creek word-ending meaning "group" or "those who" and carries a sense of unity or gathering. If "oc" is used in the sense of location, Ocmulgee could mean "gathering place" or "where we come together." From what can be determined, the word referred to an Indian town on the river and was later applied to the stream.

Vilula, perhaps the most puzzling name in Dodge County, designates a military district and a church. The name could be a corruption of a Creek Indian word, or it could be a given name. Given names are sometimes used as place names. (Helena in Telfair County was named for Helena Eastman, the wife of William Pitt Eastman.) If Vilula is a sir name, it is indeed an unusual name of an early family in Dodge County.

Chester, Roddy, Yonkers, Plainfield, and Empire, according to Victor Myrick and Donald Screws, may have been named for towns in New York (Yonkers) and Pennsylvania (Chester, Plainfield). New York is also known as the Empire State. At one time a huge sawmill, employing about 1500 people, operated in northern Dodge County. Individuals involved in management may have come from New York and Pennsylvania.

Place names come and go. Rape's Beach is a relatively new location. Indian Village on the Dodge-Pulaski line and Jump's Camp, north of Chauncey, no longer exist. What follows is a listing of Dodge County place names according to the eleven categories most commonly used in place name designation in the United States. If names have been omitted, it was not intentional.

<u>Non-Local Person</u>—Chauncey, Dodge High, Eastman, Godwinsville, Gresston, Mullin Town (a part of Chauncey, aka Mullingar), Normandale-Suomi.

Local Person or Family—Achord, Calvin, Copeland, Dempsey Church, Donaldson Crossing, Giddens School, Hargrove Crossing, Hendrix High, Joiner Creek, New Daniels Church, Old Daniels Church, Parkerson Church, Pitts, Rape's Beach, Stuckey's Mill Pond, Walton Creek, Rowland Chapel.

Natural Features—Crooked Creek, Glenwood Church, Lovely Grove Church, Middle Ground Church, Pleasant Grove Church, Pleasant Hill Church, Sugar Creek Church, Whitewater Church

Man Made Features—Cottondale (The Cotton Mill), Cross Roads, Five Points

Other or Foreign Places—Amoskeag, Milan, Rhine

Folklore—Sugar Creek (There are several stories concerning this name, most of them apocryphal.)

Human Desire or Condition—Benevolence Church, Fairhaven Church, Friendship Church, Hopewell Church, Orphans Church, Pilgrims Home Church, Sweet Home Church, New Union Church.

Indian—Ocmulgee Church, Ocmulgee River, Little Ocmulgee River

Animal, Insect, Flower or Tree—Alligator Creek, Bay Springs Church, Cypress Creek, Evergreen Church, Gum Swamp, Jay Bird Springs, Mosquito Creek, Oak Grove Church, Pine Level Church, Poplar Springs Church, Roach Branch

Unknown—Chester, Roddy, Plainfield, Yonkers, Empire, Mt. Hawken Church, Vilula Church

Ovid Vickers, October 1995

ILLUSTRATIONS

ILLUSTRATIONS

The following pages in this section offer a series of photographs secured from a variety of sources. Many of these images were taken from old newspapers, very old photographs and other material, so image quality may vary. For some of these images, the value of using an image not of the highest quality superseded the lack of perfect image quality in selecting these for the book.

Our primary aim was to collect this material into a single publication available to interested readers and future researchers.

The publisher thanks many people, most whose names are unknown, for securing and saving these images of our past, covering a period generally ranging from the late 1890s through the mid-1950s.

In 1970, the City of Eastman celebrated its Centennial. The celebration was well-organized and successful. One byproduct of the celebrations was the gathering of many photographs which were published in a special edition of the Eastman *Times-Journal*. Many of these were used here. We hope the reader will enjoy them.

William Pitt Eastman, namesake for the City of Eastman. Portrait painted by his granddaughter, Helena Ogden Campbell. The painting is displayed at the Eastman House. Mrs. Ogden donated it to the City of Eastman. (Image 1)

William E. Dodge. Statue located in New York City in Bryant Park, behind the iconic New York Public Library on 42nd Street, near Broadway. (Image 2)

A. G. Williamson monument in Orphans Church Cemetery, near Eastman. Pictured is his wife, Martha, and adopted son, Jay Gould Williamson. The monument was manufactured in Italy and shipped to the United States. The mausoleum is on the National Historic Register. (Image 3)

This house may be one of the first dwellings built in Eastman proper other than those of local farmers who settled the area. It appears to have been located along the eastern side of the railroad, across from the depot. Note the roof of the building behind the back right side of the small house, likely the depot. This location would have been on what is now the Dublin Road between the railroad and the courthouse. (Image 4)

Example of a "log pen house". The Andrew Jackson Hargrove home place, once located at Hargrove Crossing, south of Eastman, just north of Harry Hargrove Road. Standing on the porch is Nancy Hendley Hargrove, who lived to be 96, a rare feat in those days. The house was dismantled and moved to the Milan Road home place of Audrey Hargrove Cofield, great-granddaughter of Andrew Jackson and Nancy Hargrove. (Image 5)

Illustrations 119

The home of William Pitt Eastman, photographed circa 1900s, possibly earlier. Built in 1872, the nine room mansion included a connected house in the rear that was later moved. The estate included acreage containing a small farm and a manicured park open to public use. Below is a recent detail of the house. (Image 6 and Image 7)

The Uplands Hotel as it appeared to the guests who visited from all over the country in the 1870s through 1907. It was located on what is now Fifth Avenue, covering an area from Fifth to Seventh Avenue on the north, bounded on the west by Eastman Way and the east by West Main Street, next to the railroad. It boasted 100 rooms, orchestras, seasonal entertainment and assorted other activities. (Image 8)

Illustrations 121

An idealized rendition of the Uplands, taken from an invoice the hotel sent to a customer. (Image 9)

The Uplands Hotel, under construction. Note the scaffolding to the left side. The facility opened in 1876 and burned in 1907. (Image 10)

Hotel De Lietch. The Hotel was located along the railroad on the corner of East Main Street and Fourth Avenue. It was a nice establishment which catered to regular travelers as well as a temporary dwelling place for "drummers" or salesmen. A front view is shown below. Built circa 1905 and burned in 1930. (Image 11 and Image 12)

Illustrations 123

The Lee Land Hotel opened in 1926. It was located facing Fifth Avenue where College Street dead-ended. Before Oak Street was expanded from south of Fifth Avenue, the main traffic route down Highway 341 turned left at the light onto Fifth Avenue heading east, then turned right onto College Street. Before the advent of the interstate highways a steady traffic of tourists passed through Eastman. Many of them stopped off at the Lee Land Hotel.

The Lee Land was built on the same lot where the Uplands Hotel once stood. It was demolished in the late-1960s. The Citizens Bank now resides on this property. If one wonders where the hotel derived its name, it is related to William (Billy) Lee, a farmer whose land comprised the area on which Eastman was built. There is also a Lee voting district honoring his memory. Postcards of the hotel depicting it through the years may be found on online auction sites.

The photograph above depicts the hotel probably in the early 1950s. Note the neon sign atop the hotel (barely visible) and the metal/neon sign out front on the right side of the picture. (Image 13)

Pictured above is the original Dodge County Courthouse, probably in its later years. William Pitt Eastman donated the land on which it was built. It was dedicated in 1874 by William E. Dodge, who donated funds for its construction. It was Dodge's only visit to Eastman. The reported amount he donated varies from $15,000 to $25,000, a large sum at that time. In return, the county was named after him. This building was demolished to make way for the new courthouse which opened in 1904.

In the novel Lightwood by Brainard Cheney, set in the early days of Dodge County and the timber wars, there is a scene depicting the gathering to hear William E. Dodge dedicate the new courthouse. Cheney did extensive research for the historical novel and his story of this event rings true. One character tells his parent excitedly: "Look, Pa. It's painted." (Image 14)

Illustrations 125

The second and most impressive of the three Dodge County courthouses. It boasted entrances on all four sides, an impressive dome, columns and other beautiful design work by architect E. C. Hosford, a native of Eastman. Each week, the clock was reset to the correct time, as the community depended on it as its standard time source. Regrettably, this beautiful building burned in 1939.

The third courthouse was built on the foundations of this building, using some of the exterior as well. It no longer featured a dome. As of 2019, the courthouse in inoperable and a remodeling or replacement is being considered by the county officials and community. (Image 15)

126 Selected Sketches of Dodge County, Georgia History

Street scenes in Eastman circa 1910. Top view shows West Main toward the Depot, seen in the center distance. In the foreground is a well placed in the middle of the unpaved street. DeLietch Hotel is visible at right side. (Image 16)

Below is further down the street, at the depot and Fifth Avenue. Two story building is the post office, later Masonic Lodge and Periwinkle Tea Room. (Image 17 below)

Illustrations 127

Eastman Cotton Mill, incorporated in 1905 by local businessmen. St. Clair Smyly was contracted as superintendent. It was located on the north side of town at 14th Avenue and the railroad. A community named Cottondale served as home for many of the workers. Below is a load of cotton on its way to the cotton gin. (Image 18 and Image 19)

The Eastman Post Office pre-1936. Located on West Main Street at the corner of Fifth Avenue. The two-story building later held a Masonic Hall and the Periwinkle Tea Room. It was torn down in the 1970s. In this photograph, it was decorated for a parade, likely a July 4th celebration. This Post Office facility was replaced in 1936 by the post office on the next page. (Image 20)

Illustrations   129

Post Office located on West Main at corner of Fourth Avenue. Built in 1936 as a WPA project. This facility was replaced in 1989 by the current post office located on Second Avenue. (Image 21)

Former site of the Eastman Bus Station and Western Union facility, now owned by the City of Eastman. It is on the Historic Register. It was run for many years by Mrs. Annie Wilbanks, who was an institution in town. At that time, many packages were shipped via Greyhound buses. Located on College Street near Second Avenue. (Image 22)

Millinery and clothing store on Main Street in Eastman. Martha Sheldon, the niece of Ms. Brown, worked for her, making hats. She later opened a florist shop. Note the window display. (Image 23)

Coleman Hardware circa 1920s with crowd gathered to win the truck being given away. Coleman's is still in business in 2019, with a different variety of items for sale. (Image 24)

REMEMBRANCES
OF DAYS GONE BY

MEMORY OF A DAY IN 1926

I remember so well a special day of my life when I was in the fourth grade. I began to feel ill on that day and when you don't feel good, all a little girl wants to do is go home. The procedure to leave the school during school time was completely different from the way it is today. I simply went to the teacher and told her that I felt sick and wanted to go home. She gave me permission to leave immediately.

So, I began what seemed to me like an endless journey. When I left the school I walked up the sidewalk of College Street toward town for three blocks. When I reached Second Avenue I turned to the right and within one short block there was on my left the Christian Church on the corner of Second and Main Streets. My journey continued down Main Street which faced the railroad. After the Church the Ford Agency was next and then the fire station, police department, city hall and then the Bank of Eastman on the corner of Third and Main.

The next block had some vacant buildings but to the best of my memory, a grocery store was on the corner and next to it were two small stores, Wilkinson Jewelry and a barber shop. Wynn's Department Store sold an assortment of things but the Ten Cent Store next door was where my purchases were made. A drug store was next door but I can't remember the name and then there was Harris' Department Store where I had bought some pretty shoes. Berg's Department Store was next and Ideal Pharmacy was on the corner of Fourth Avenue.

By this time I was very tired so I sat awhile on the edge of the brick sidewalk and settled my feet on the dark dusty unpaved road. It always interested me to look at the tall Confederate Monument in the center of where Fourth Avenue and Main Streets met. The monument was so tall.

I crossed Fourth Avenue and continued down Main Street. The first store was a grocery store and next was Levine's Department Store where I had seen so many pretty dresses in the window. I traveled on past Hardin Supply, Anderson and Leonard, Citizens Bank and Edwards Furniture Store. A hotel entrance was next but the hotel was upstairs, then there was a barber shop and finally the Periwinkle Tea Room. In the basement of this building the Times-Journal paper was published.

I walked along all these blocks until I reached the small city park at the end of town. I knew this park well for I went through it daily on my way to and from school. The Lee Land Hotel was on the left side of the park but I headed toward the depot side of the park. I went down the steps to the park sidewalk which led to the marble benches that surrounded an ornate fountain that honored William Pitt Eastman. Here, I decided to lie down and take a nap and since I was so bundled up in my heavy winter coat and warm cap I was not cold. I fell into a long nap and the next thing I knew my classmate was calling to me to wake up. The school day was over and I was not feeling fine. We walked home together. When Mama came home from work it never occurred to me to tell her about my unusual day.

The park was always a special beauty spot for me. It was there that I saw my first Japanese Magnolia Tree in bloom. I didn't know its name but I thought it was the most beautiful thing I had ever seen.

The cement steps leading into the park eventually became covered with soil. Later the public library was built in the park and it was during this time that the old cement steps were uncovered. There was a write-up in the local paper about this discovery. I knew the steps were there all along because I used them for eleven years that I went to and from the schoolhouse.

Now, as I drive by the park, it is with a warm feeling that I remember that little girl taking a long nap on the marble bench in that beautiful little park.

Irene Gregory, March 28, 1996

Comment: Irene Gregory was an elementary school teacher at Eastman Elementary School from the 1950s until the 1970s, when she retired. She was a much-admired educator and respected citizen of the community.

EASTMAN BAKERY

In 1951, Ralph and Aurelia Johns opened their first business—a bakery. It was in a building on College Street which was owned by Mr. Lee Studstill. Trust was something to be valued back then. Sometimes Mr. Lee would come in to buy some doughnuts around the first of the month and we'd tell him to wait a few minutes so we could write his rent check. He'd most always say, "I don't have time to bother with that now; when I want my rent money I'll come get it." Sometimes he'd wait two or three months before collecting. We'd tell him we'd rather pay on time for fear we might not have it later. He'd just laugh and say, "I ain't worried." But we knew for a fact that he'd walk by our front door and go two doors down and collect rent the first day of each month on another building he owned.

In 1955 on February 1 we moved our bakery to Main Street where there were more people walking by and more stores. That was before shopping centers and malls began. Every business in Eastman was downtown, not scattered out as it is now.

We rented this building from Rev. Judson Burrell, who still owns the building today. His wife inherited the building from her father, T. H. Edwards. Business was good even though we had to make everything we sold. We think the main reason for our good business was that we used good ingredients, fresh eggs, milk, and everything fresh, no prepared mixes of any kind.

Our two children, Karen and Myron, grew up helping out. Even when they both attended the University of Georgia, they helped us during the summer vacations and holidays.

The bakery business called for long hours and early rising to get all of the doughnut dough and everything else that used yeast to rise. We tried to have fresh doughnuts, cakes, pies, cookies, and sandwiches by 7:30 each morning. When we opened the front door there were usually people waiting to get in.

The largest cake we ever made weighed 464 pounds. It was made for Holcomb Super Market which had just opened in the building between Buck's Grill and Horne Funeral Home. The occasion was a grand opening of the store. We made another 350 pound cake that was ordered from Hawkinsville for some large occasion. One week-end we made seven wedding cakes plus many birthday cakes.

We joked about our business "going to the dogs." For eleven years we made a cake for a dog's birthday. We always wrote Happy Birthday Baby on it and it was a pound cake since that was what the dog liked best. After eleven years the dog died.

We worked hard, enjoyed a good business. Therefore, when Ralph reached age 65 we decided to retire and see how it was to sleep a little later.

On March 17, 1978, we sold our bakery and found that it is great to get up at a decent hour. We miss seeing people and serving good doughnuts. We made 250 dozen each Saturday and 100 dozen each week day. We also miss our help, three helpers in the kitchen and two salesgirls. It was a good business and a good life.

Aurelia Johns

Comment: The Eastman Bakery was an institution in Eastman for many years. The Johns Family were exceptionally nice people and very hard workers.

REMEMBERING THE KANSAS CITY SPECIALS

Perhaps the most poignant paragraph in the new *History of Dodge County* (1994) is William John Steele's description of the meeting of the last Kansas City Specials at Gresston in 1967. Because our home in Godwinsville was only 30 yards from the main line, I grew up being taken up into engines by men like engineer Alan Rabey and conductor Crowel Bazemore. I listened for the train, watched for the train, waved at the train, and rode the train until I grew up and went away to school. Each time I read Steele's words, I am filled with nostalgia. Steele says:

"Trains Nos. 7 and 8, the KC Specials made the final run on a cold winter's night in 1967. Meeting at the Gresston passing track at 2:23 A.M. with extra blasts of their whistles, brightening and dimming of their headlights, and waves of lanterns, the KC Specials saluted each other in passing with their 98-year ritual of meeting. Then they glided into that great Valhalla of history. Their final meeting was in Dodge County, as surely, God must have intended."

Today no matter where I am, I always think of the Kansas City Specials when I hear a train blow somewhere in the distance. The following poem expresses my feelings about trains.

NIGHT TRAIN

By

Ovid Vickers

Long, low and lonesome,
The whistle woke me.
Bundled in a blanket,
I went to the window.

In the still November night
The headlamp washed the dark,
Reflecting on steel ribbons
Stretching away toward morning.

A rush of drive wheels blurred
Beyond our front yard fence.
Passengers breathed away the night
Coach windows framing sleeping faces.
All those childhood nights,
Keeping an "on time" schedule.
The train took with it those years
Before I left my father's house.

ANTICIPATION

One lazy July afternoon,
as sunlight caught
the wings of dragonflies
and heat shimmered
above the wire grass,
I went with Bill Charles
across the back forty.

We passed
the sun bleached bones
of some long dead cow,
painted tattoos on our arms
with purple pokeberries,
and walked from sunshine
into cypress shade.

Schools of silver minnows
stirred sand at the creek's edge
while water iris stood tall,
pointing to loops and coils
of yellow trumpet vine
embracing the lower limbs
of tulip trees.

Bill Charles threw stones
at a squirrel,
and I ate a handful
of huckleberries.
We shed our clothes,
looked at each other
for signs of manhood,
and dived from a cypress stump.

Ovid Vickers, January 1996

CHRISTMAS MEMORIES

Justin Bracewell

When I was growing up as the son of a textile worker during the "Great Depression" years, living was quite difficult at times. My daddy's health failed him while he was still young and this contributed significantly to our shortage of luxuries. The childhood Christmas that I remember most was that year when I got a cap pistol but no caps. In order to shoot it and make noise, I would use the heads of wooden matches. However, I did not feel particularly deprived because every one of my companions was in about the same situation. As an adult, one of the most difficult Christmas times I can recall occurred when the Cotton Mill shut down just before Christmas. I had two small children, Ronald, age 3 and Robert, age 1. I did not know where we were going to get money to buy Santa Claus gifts that year, but I almost always did. I raised chickens and had eggs. So I sold 30 chickens "off the yard" to Buck and Lila Gilbert who operated the White House Café on Main Street in Eastman. I used this money to get Santa Claus for the boys. The most joyous Christmas which I remember was in 1964. My wife and I had just built a new house and the children and grandchildren were all there.

Mary Jean Bracewell

When I stop to recall Christmas memories there are two that make an impression on me. The first memory occurred when I was around six years old. Santa Claus brought me a doll, doll bed, pillow, and sheets, and a bed spread, all lovingly made by my mother. I also got a table and chairs and tea set. It was my first Christmas memory. I always got a rubber ball but it usually did not last longer than Christmas Day. Being the youngest and only girl with four brothers, they have always preferred playing with my ball than with what they got! That year, Santa Claus brought my mother a small and inexpensive set of vases. I could not understand why I had gotten so much and she so little, but I realized later how unselfish my mother was.

Another Christmas memory occurred a year or two later. We used fireplaces for heat and all of these were very small. I was very upset about how Santa Claus was going to climb down the chimney when it was so small. Mother and Daddy assured me, however, that Santa Claus always made a way to get in and that they would be sure to leave the door on the front porch unlocked and when he found he could not come down the chimney that he would come through the door. I was satisfied with this before I went to bed. This particular year I got a new bathrobe and bedroom slippers. Years later mother told me that she tried them on me after I went to sleep.

Bertie Mae Garrett

I am glad that Martha [Saunders] asked me to reminisce upon this subject. Only a few days before her plans were revealed, I decided to clean out the bottom drawer of a chest of drawers. There she was—the subject of this memorable Christmas!

The year was long ago, possibly three-score ten or more. Yet, I was looking at a beautiful little China doll in her original Santa Claus box that I received on a special Christmas. Several things happened to me, a tiny little underweight girl, about the same Santa Claus of this year.

I was a first-grader and cried all the way home from school in North Augusta as I walked behind my two smart older sisters. I was bringing home a white report card while they had their usual blue card. Blue meant very good in everything; white was only average, but better than red, and I liked the red one that I usually received. They tried to convince me that white was better and prettier than the red one. Later, maybe the same afternoon, I was caught playing near the trolley track which was not far from our front door steps. I had been reprimanded and cautioned never to do this. But I did! And this time, the conductor stopped the trolley, got out, spanked me severely, and set me down on our doorstep. Mama took over from there.

I remember going up the stairs of our "little pink doll house" as we called it, and crying myself to sleep, thinking that Santa Claus and no one else loved me. In the early morning, my sister woke me holding a doll in her hand. "Look what Santa left in your box." It was, and is, the most beautiful dolly I had ever seen. I grabbed her in my arms and started running to the stairs to see what else Santa had brought me. Maybe my gown tripped me, or I just fell over my own feet, but down the stairs I tumbled to the first landing. Their Dolly and I both lay broken, she with a cracked shoulder and I with bruises and tears.

My Dad tried to repair her with glue, but to this day Blondie, my dolly, has not healed and her beautiful blond curls are leaving her head and settling in the box. After all, she is now nearly as old as I am. Even with the fall on the stairs, the broken dolly, the spanking, and the academic deficiency of my initial schooling, it was a Christmas that I remember well.

Tom Harton

One Christmas memory still amuses me when I think of it. The year, which may not be precisely accurate, was, we shall say, 1920. My father developed an overwhelming interest in chickens, Rhode Island reds in particular. I might add that he later won a number of blue ribbons for his chickens at the State Fair. Eventually he had two chicken houses in the back yard, wired for electricity so he could wake up the chickens during the night to lay eggs, believing this would increase production. He went even further. There were about seven in our household at the time but this did not deter him from setting up an incubator in my bedroom.

That Christmas began in the customary manner with a highly decorated tree, including strings of real popcorn, and a collection of gift packages under the tree. Most were wrapped in the customary Christmas style except one group. They were the gifts my father gave to the children (three of us at the time, ages 14, 11 and 8). His gifts were always placed under the tree between our bedtime and the wee small hours of the morning. He went through the pretense of loosely wrapping our presents in brown paper, not tied. As we children pounced on the unidentified presents he announced who they were for.

This Christmas went according to plan for some minutes and then there was an interruption. My father had checked the incubator and discovered the chicks were about ready to enter the world. He pushed the panic button and we spent the rest of Christmas morning (each of us) cracking shells and easing the new chicks into a marvelous world.

Victor Myrick

My mother, Nellie Harrell Myrick, told me this when she was past 80 years old. It happened about 1914. I'm writing it as she told it.

"One Christmas it had rained all day every day for a week. Papa kept telling us that if it didn't stop so he could go to town we might not get any Christmas presents. Well, it didn't stop, so after dinner on Christmas Eve he hitched the mules to the wagon and said he was going to the store at Baileys Park. This was about a mile from our house. All four of us girls slept in two double beds in the same room. After we went to bed we whispered a lot about whether or not we would have presents the next morning. About daylight one of my sisters slipped out of the bedroom and peeped into the dining room where we had each placed a box for our gifts. She woke us all up and said she thought we each had a big doll. This caused real excitement. In a little while Mama came in and told us to get up and see what we had. It was a big disappointment when we found we each had a roll of red cloth for a new dress. But we got excited when we lifted the cloth up and found under it a little wooden trunk to keep small items in and some apples, oranges, and candy. It was a good Christmas after all."

Cece Saunders

I remember the annual Fifth Avenue Christmas Tree Burning. Flashing sparks and pungent evergreen smoke floated to the chilled sky as we children were reconfirmed each New Year's Eve. It is the warmth and holiday love found in a neighborhood gathered around a bonfire that I hold as a very special Christmas memory. It was the annual giant Christmas tree burning and hot dog roast that our neighborhood families shared the last day of each December. The grown-ups had the mundane task of preparing the food, setting up some shaky tables and counting out the marshmallows for roasting. We children, the Coffees, the Whighams, the Jarrards, the Saunders, the Smiths, the McCranies and the McDaniels had the herculean task of collecting the fuel for the annual bonfire—dozens and dozens of the undecorated Christmas trees that were thrown out on December 31st! (Thank goodness the old wives tale predicted "bad luck" if the Christmas tree was left standing after the 31st.)

The Schwinn bike wheels whirred and we giggled with out-of-school abandon as the discarded balsam and fir trees were collected from the street curbs, tied to our rear bike fenders, and pulled to the dead end patch of asphalt that defined our world on the west end of Fifth Avenue. This is the Fifth Avenue before the trees were cut down, the stream re-channeled and the pastures turned into building lots. Fifth Avenue ended in front of my house, providing us with the perfect collection point for the mountains of discarded trees.

You can well imagine the incendiary quality of these dried evergreens! We filled the air with our *"ohhs"* and *"ahhs"* as each of us took turns tossing trees onto the bonfire. Our Moms and Dads, seated on aluminum lawn chairs, encircled the giant bonfire. The boughs crackled and shot flames into the air. Inevitably, the Fire Department would be called by some far-off sighting of a great conflagration on Fifth Avenue. The fire trucks would arrive and the firemen would laugh as they remembered that, yet again, the Fifth Avenue Christmas Tree Burning was in progress.

The evenings' festivities also included a rousing game of 'hide 'n seek'. I always ran for the spidery and damp crawl space under our house, crouching next to the lawnmower until I was caught.

At the end of the evening, we were often gathered into a kid-sized circle to hear a chilling story of the escapades of Jingles and Jangles. Those walking and talking skeletons were the creation of "Miss Julia" Smith, our neighbor and friend from up the street. Surrounded as we were by closing night sounds and the dying embers of the spent trees, her scary tale was an extra special treat for us all.

Chester Saunders

Chester Saunders was about ten years old when he received his first bicycle. A few days before Christmas he was standing at the Helena depot and saw a grand red and white bicycle being unloaded. It was crated and he dared not look at the name but he says that "he knew in his heart that it was his." As he hoped it would be, it was under the tree on Christmas morning. Also this bicycle was special because it had coaster brakes, one of the newest additions to bicycle technology. Coaster brakes allowed the wheels to turn while the pedals were motionless. This particular bicycle looms large in his memory.

Martha Saunders

Fleeting flashes of memory can be unbelievable in retrospect. When Martha Saunders was a pre-school child, she remembers one Christmas tree which was fairyland in beauty. The tree was large, full dark green and, of course, personally cut by the family members. What was so remarkable were the tiny real candles fastened at the end of each branch. These candles were all being lighted for Christmas. She has always wondered how so many little candles could burn at one time. Nobody seemed to worry about fire.

Ovid Vickers

In the years before power lines laced rural Dodge County those who lived in the country would often go to Eastman on Christmas Eve. Some last minute shopping was done and children could see the brightly colored lights strung from pole to pole along the streets, the decorated doors of homes, and the Christmas trees shining brightly through "front room" windows.

In the mid-1940s a near miracle happened. The REA put up poles and strung electric wires like a giant web across the entire county. In the bright light of an electric bulb, we decorated our tree with handmade garlands of bright construction paper, strings of popcorn, and sweetgum balls covered with foil from gum wrappers.

At noon, my father caught a ride to town. Dark was approaching when he re-appeared, carrying a large brown bag. My sister and I were asked to bring in some stove wood for the next day. When we had stacked the wood on the back porch, we opened the door to behold a tree covered with lights—not just ordinary lights, but lights that bubbled and twinkled and dazzled.

I don't remember the gifts I got that Christmas, but I do remember that my father showed his love for us with a few strands of lights to illuminate a Christmas tree. Now, after all these years, that love still shines in the far recesses of my mind.

November 1995

CULTURE, LEISURE, THE ARTS AND COMMUNITY LIFE IN DODGE COUNTY

EASTMAN POST OFFICE MURAL

The WPA (Works Progress Administration) projects of the 1930s were undertaken by the New Deal in an effort to stimulate the economy. Projects in many areas were begun to give work to artists, architects, archeologists, and other professionals along with unemployed workers in general. The average person of today associates WPA projects with a road or a bridge. However, the most important WPA project in Eastman was the mural in the Eastman Post Office. In 1989 the Postmaster, Stan McDaniel, incorporated an extra task in association with the new post office building by repairing and transferring the old mural from the former post office. He contracted with a company from Texas to carry out this task.

The paint on the mural had begun to peel and there was also difficulty in removing it since the canvas was glued to the wall. The mural was gone for nearly a year and, when returned, the paint had been restored and the mural framed for immediate hanging. The name of the mural is "Georgia Lumbermen Receiving Mail."

The New Deal made walls available not only in schools and government buildings, but in libraries, hospitals, prisons, and other tax-supported institutions as well which had never previously contained such features.

There is a distinctive sense of history in these murals. Besides the question of establishing the mural as a harmonious part of the architecture, the artist also had to make it a part of the community. The post office was envisioned as a social center frequented by almost everyone and there were three broad category subjects: the postal service, local scenes and local history. Each artist was urged wherever possible to visit the community for which his mural was destined.

Murals under the WPA sponsorship were placed primarily in institutions in the largest areas of the country. The murals in the post offices were spread across the State in small towns, resort areas, and agricultural centers. The mural competitions were administered directly from Washington. Most of the smaller post office commissions were awarded to the runners-up in the large competitions.

One can assume that the artist, whose signature is illegible, planned his painting without a visit to our area. Otherwise why would he paint mountains in the upper left area of the scene? Also, local people who are familiar with the proper way to carry an axe will observe the axe blade turned in the wrong direction on the man's shoulder. However, since the great pine trees were the foundational wealth of this area, it is appropriate that the workers are shown as lumbermen.

Most murals in the 1930s were oil on canvas, affixed to the wall. This was partly because of the high cost of a true fresco. Oil on canvas, on the other hand, could be painted in the studio, then brought to the building and applied to the wall in one day. Also, these murals were considered removable and, therefore, appropriate to buildings that might be tax-supported, but not government owned. The cost for both materials and labor for the WPA murals averaged about $14.00 per square foot. The Eastman mural has 63 square feet of area which would have totaled about $882.00.

When you next visit the Eastman post office, take a minute to appreciate the mural that we have.

Contributed by Stan McDaniel, Retired Postmaster, Eastman, Georgia, with information from the Smithsonian Institute

Comment: The mural is mounted on the wall behind the counter at the Eastman Post Office on Second Avenue.

A HISTORY IN STITCHES

Quilting has become an art form. Today material for squares and stripping is bought with great care so that the colors and patterns coordinate. The quilt must be in harmony with the color scheme and décor of the room where it will be displayed. A modern quilt is seldom bought or made for a utilitarian purpose; instead the quilt is a display item.

There was a time when the majority of the quilts pieced and quilted in Dodge County were used for keeping warm in winter. On a cold January night, after the lamp had been blown out and the fire had "died down," quilts were a necessity.

In the 1920s and 1930s it was not uncommon for six or eight women to gather in the home of a neighbor and spend the day quilting. The quilting was the culmination of a process described as piecing and stripping. First, a pattern was selected. The most common patterns were the Flower Garden, Step Around the Mountain, Dutch Girl, Dresden Plate, The Fan, Double Wedding Ring, and if the material for cutting squares was not wide enough to accommodate the pattern, what was known as a String Quilt could be made. Some quilt tops were embroidered. Church ladies often embroidered the names of members of a congregation on a solid white top, or names of family members would be embroidered at the bottoms of squares. New overalls were often overly long. When the legs were cut off and hemmed, this material was saved and sometimes sewn into a quilt top.

Cloth for cutting squares could be secured in a number of ways. Before World War II flour was often sold in sacks made of print material. Cow feed also could be bought in print sacks. These prints were carefully washed and ironed to be used for quilt squares. All scraps from the making of a dress were saved, and Sears and Roebuck sold what was called a "scrap bundle." The scrap bundle sold for about fifty cents and contained enough material to make a quilt.

Quilts were suspended for quilting in two ways. One method was to suspend the frames on four ropes attached to rings in the ceiling. The other method was to place the quilt on a frame which sat on the floor. If a quilt was suspended from the ceiling, eight women could quilt. A floor frame would accommodate only three quilters to each side Quilting was done either by the square or in what were called shells or straight lines that intersected.

The owner of the quilt was expected to serve dinner to the quilters. This meal was comparable to what country folks called "Sunday dinner." Fried chicken was usually served along with several vegetables, hot biscuits, iced tea, and chocolate or coconut cake.

A quilting served two purposes. It not only served as a means of getting a quilt completed, but it also served as an opportunity for community visiting. Family histories were given, old stories were retold, and community happenings such as births, deaths, marriages, crop failures, the weather, and good gardens were discussed from every angle.

I can remember as a small child going with my mother to quiltings in the Godwinsville community. These were special days because if a child was quiet he or she could sit in the room with the quilters and listen to the stories, comments, and gossip. About mid afternoon all the children were given another piece of cake or pie, and that made the day very special.

Ovid Vickers

GIRL'S BASKETBALL AT EASTMAN HIGH, 1931-1933

Girl's basketball [*as it is described locally*] has always been an important sport in Dodge County. Many of the older citizens of Eastman who are still living remember with great clarity and interest the special years of 1930–1933. There were two seasons when the Eastman girls were undefeated and many times the score was over 100.

During these early years the girl's game was different from today in that the two centers had to tip off the ball in the middle of the court after each goal. Team members played on only one-half of the court and could not cross the center line onto the other side. This consumed time which prevented a fast build-up of points. It is reported that during the games the girls frequently managed to score more than four points per minute thereby creating a winning game.

The articles that follow from the *Times-Journal* gave an enthusiastic report on each game and usually referred to the girls as the Eastman lassies. The team seemed to play nearby communities more frequently such as Chauncey, but the championship required playing in all of the challenging towns in the Third District.

We must also remember that the transportation was more of an issue than it is in our current times. The team traveled in Model T Ford Blue Bird busses that had wooden bodies. You can be sure that flat tires were a problem. However, the teams were traveling in the best available and probably never worried one bit.

1931-1932 Season

"The Eastman girls swamped the lassies of McRae-Helena by 44 to 12 in the first game of the '31-'32 season. Players were R. Whigham, A. L. Jones, B. Jimmerson, O. Rawlins, and Cranford. The return trip of the McRae-Helena team to Eastman within the month was exciting. It was evident that the visitors intended to win the game but the Eastman girls intended to have the final say which they did with the 60 to 12 score. E. Woodard was added as a player.

A special event is recorded with the team visiting in Atlanta in February 1932. They paid a visit to the State capitol, had their picture taken with the governor, attended the Fox theater, took in the sights of Grant's Park, Stone Mountain and other points of interest and then on Saturday night "mopped up" the Jonesboro basketball team who were said to be the champions of that section of Georgia. The girls won by a score of 76 to 11.

This was the first game lost by the Jonesboro girls on their home court in three years."

The next home game was with Pitts with the Eastman girls in control, winning by a score of 67 to 11.

The reporters of the *Times-Journal* give an interesting account of the Baxley and Eastman game as follows: "The Baxley Pirate lassies ventured over to the Eastman Wildcats den on last Friday night. Although bold enough to come into the Wildcat's domain, they didn't bring sufficient strength with them to capture or to put the Wildcats on the defensive.

"The Eastman lassies had heard that the Baxley Pirates were very strong. With this in mind, they began the game with high spirit and hopes for a close game. Finding little opposition, the Eastmanites scored at will from the first whistle until the half when the score was 37 to 0.

Substitutes were put in for the third quarter and Baxley scored two points on foul shots. During the fourth quarter the larger Wildcats were put back into the affray and they inflicted more scratches making a total score of 51 to 2."

The next month the Eastman girls won the tournament in Hawkinsville and set a total record of 201 to 33. As the *Times-Journal* reported: "The Eastman quintet had been setting a pace all season that other teams admired. Cordele withdrew from the tournament just in time to keep out of the path of the Wildcats. Then up hopped Vienna but down she flopped by a score of 97 to 12. Chauncey tried Eastman out Saturday morning to see if she could defeat the Wildcats. But Chauncey tried and that was all because Eastman put them away by a score of 66 to 12.

"Then on Saturday night was when the fun began. The lassies from Byron were brought into the finals to try to entertain the Eastmanites. At the end of the first quarter Byron was leading by two points, due to a hold up in the Eastman goal shooting, but at that point the Wildcats let out for a stretch and at the end of the half were in the lead by three points 16 to 13. During the half, Coach Long must have told the girls a few things because as soon as they went back into the game they began to sink 'em from every angle of the court and in a few minutes had a score of 38 to 14. At this stage of the game, the referee suggested that the game be called on account of the court was wet from leaks in the roof."

The 1931-1932 season ended with a total of 1,283 points to their opponent's 261, or an average of 56 points per game to 12 for their opponents. This proved to all that the Wildcats were the best in the State.

1932—1933 Season

"The past season's champions started a new year by playing Jeffersonville in early November. They settled down to playing at the first whistle and on the first toss up they chalked up a goal. The Eastmanites showed great skill in the passing team work and even in the scoring ability which resulted in more than four points per minute. The team beginning this year was R. Whigham, S. McKinnon, A. L. Jones, O. Cranford, I. Stuckey, and L. Harrell.

"The old favorite competition, Chauncey, returned for a game on Nov. 24 and the game was exciting and ended with Eastman as winner. Coach Paul Long announced that he had several open dates and would be glad to meet all comers in games of basketball, as he believed that the Eastman team was well along the road to championship that year.

"The fast girls team form Hazlehurst came over to Eastman to see if they could defeat the Eastman lassies but they could not hold a pace equal to that of the Wildcats. The final score was 80 to 8.

"Coach Long's girls, champions of the Third District, and undefeated for the past several seasons kept up their record by defeating the Hawkinsville girls 131 to 2 in the first game of the season and again with a score of 101 to 8. The Eastman lassies defeated the Alamo team by 37 to 13 and the Pitts girls by 95 to 7. The first team players are about the same who are Whigham, McKinnon, Jones, Cranford, Stuckey, Harrell, Coley.

"The girl's basketball tournament for the eastern section of the Third District was held on Eastman court March 2, 3, and 4. The Eastman team, champions of the Third District last season and undefeated this season, was getting into shape to fight for another championship.

"The semi-finals left Byron and Eastman to contest for first place. Eastman took an early lead although Byron held the Eastman girls to the lowest score of the season which was 28 to 15.

"The Eastman High School basketball girls, by reason of having been the winner in the eastern division of the Third District and a forfeit from Cusseta, the winner of the western division, claims the championship of the Third District.

"The Eastman girls have not lost a game in three years and their score in 23 games amounts to about 1,600 points. They announce that they are ready to play any high school girl's team anywhere and anytime.

This team was awesome."

(Information taken from the Times-Journal issues of 1930-1933)

MINSTREL SHOWS IN DODGE COUNTY

On a clear mid-autumn day during the cotton picking season when money was sure to be available, the brightly painted railroad cars with banners announcing "Silas Green from New Orleans" would roll into the Eastman sidetrack. A week or two later another company, "Woolcott's Rabbit Foot Minstrels" would arrive in a caravan of five or six busses and several moving vans.

As soon as possible, a big tent was pitched at the old fairgrounds on the western edge of town. This tent held a large portable stage and seating for several hundred people. Because these shows were composed of all black cast members and because integration was some years in the future, the seating was arranged with a center aisle. Whites sat on the right and blacks on the left.

The evening's show was preceded by a parade. From the depot on down College Street to the old Bank of Eastman where a right turn was made onto Second Avenue, the parade headed toward the fairgrounds. Black and white citizens gathered and freely mingled and jostled each other for the best viewing places.

Once the crowd had gathered and anticipation reached its peak, expectant ears could hear in the distance the fanfare of trumpets followed by the rhythmic cadence of drums signaling the beginning of the parade. After what seemed hours of waiting, one could see in the distance the parade master in his brightly colored uniform leading the performers in step to a brisk march. As they marched by Levine's Department Store or the College Street Pharmacy, the magic of it all was wonderful to my ten year old eyes. The *café au lait* show girls, the slick-haired men in handsome suits, the bandsmen in their gaudy uniforms, and the comics in their ridiculous costumes prancing to the sounds of enchanted instruments was almost too much for my eyes, ears, and mind to comprehend.

The evening performances under the big tent were filled with spirited dancing, jazz and blues songs, and several stand-up comics. The comics often made fun of prominent Eastman citizens, both black and white. The Hamilton Funeral Home and local white doctors were often the butt of a comic's jokes.

Such black stars as Gertrude "Ma" Rainey, Jelly Roll Morton, and Bessie Smith performed in Eastman with the Silas Green shows long before they gained a national reputation as entertainers.

The minstrel show had its beginnings before the Civil War by white performers who painted their faces black. It was 1865 before the first permanent all-black company was established when W.H. Lee organized the Georgia

Minstrels with a group of fifteen ex-slaves in Macon. Minstrels continued to be a popular form of entertainment until the late 1930s. There are many reasons for the demise of the minstrel shows. World War II, television, and a changed attitude, by both the black and white communities, toward the minstrel type of dancing, singing and humor certainly contributed to the minstrel's inability to continue attracting an audience.

The minstrel show is gone. But as a young boy in Dodge County, I was entranced by the music, awed by the colorful costumes, and convulsed by the comedians. "The minstrel show is coming." "You going?" "I saw a poster high up on the side of Mr. Jessup's warehouse saying Silas Green will be in Eastman next Thursday." Such statements are now merely echoes and memories of Dodge County in a younger time.

Ovid Vickers, September 28, 1995

TIDBITS FROM THE *EASTMAN TIMES*

The *Eastman Times* was organized in 1873 with R.S. Burton as proprietor and H.W. J. Ham as editor. In five months the paper announced a total of 400 subscribers. For the first few years the news consisted of reprints from the world news, full page stories and articles from other sources. Gradually the local area news was printed but all along there was advertising of businesses, lawyers, and sheriff's sales in Dodge County. Excerpts from the paper follow:

"The post-office has been a source of problems from the beginning—March 1874 Postal Reform—It is said that the Senate Appropriations Committee will propose an amendment to the laws so as to provide that after the 30th of June, 1874, means of transportation in the mails of samples of merchandise, packages of clothing, seeds, cuttings, bulbs, roots, scions, samples of metals, ores and mineralogical specimens and bound books shall cease and all laws authorizing such conveyance shall be repealed.

"The reason for such repeal is that the mails are lumbered with, among other things,, beehives, with live bees in them fed with honey and sheltered by glass, boots and shoes and other incongruous articles which are sent through the mails under the provision that everything except some dangerous liquids can be sent through the mails if not weighing over four pounds."

In the February, 1880 issue another article concerning the Eastman post office was printed.

"Major C. R. Armstrong, our clever and attentive Postmaster, has fitted up the post office with lock boxes, nickel plate sunken-die numbers, repaint and varnish, giving it a tasty, handsome, and it is said by strangers, even a city-like appearance.

"The lock boxes have all been taken, and the demand is so great the Major A. informs us that he is going to add quite a number more new ones to supply the demand. In connection with this we will also state that he thinks he will soon perfect arrangements by which this will be made a money order office."

In the June, 1874 issue:

"A Missouri man who swapped wives with another Missourian got a cow, a calf, thirty good steel traps and four children to boot."

In 1879 as the Methodist Church was nearly completed, a notice in the paper stated that additional horse racks were being added for those who had to ride to church.

In the personals of 1880:

"Three Eastman women went to Chauncey to visit a friend and *gallooped* all the way back to Eastman—which was ten miles."

In the course of researching another item it was interesting to learn about chinaberry trees. Two kinds were imported to the southern part of the U.S. and they were the regular, leggy shape and the umbrella which is a lovely shape for shade. Chinaberries were important to the early farmers and used in several ways. Dried berries were mixed with dried corn to keep the weevils out; a medicine was prepared from the berries to give to mules who had colic; and sausages were smoked with green chinaberry wood. And, of course, the children used chinaberries in their home made pop guns.

In 1879 a notice stated that the Jail House was completed and formally accepted by the County.

In 1875 an article was included which was quite typical for that time:

WHAT TO TEACH THE GIRLS

Give them a good common school education. Teach them to cook a sensible meal. Teach them to wash, iron, darn stockings, sew on buttons, make their own clothes, and a decent skirt. Teach them to bake bread and that a good kitchen saves many a cent from the apothecary. Teach them that one dollar is worth one hundred cents and that he alone is saving who spends less than his income and that all others who spend more must finally become poor. Teach them that a calico dress paid for looks better than a silk one with debts. Teach them that one round plump face is worth more than fifty consumptive beauties. Teach then to wear good strong shoes. Teach them to make purchases then calculate whether the bill accords. Teach them that they best serve the divine image by wearing tight corsets. Teach them plain common sense, to trust in and help themselves by industry. Teach them that one honest mechanic in shirt sleeves, although without a cent of property, is worth more than a dozen richly clad and *hifalutin* idlers. Teach them to work in the garden and to enjoy free nature. If circumstances will permit, teach them music, painting and all the fine arts, but give them to understand that they are matters of secondary importance. Teach them that promenading walks are better than drives and that the wild flowers, indeed, are full of beauty for him who attentively considers them. Teach them to despise the mere appearance of things and that whenever they say yea or nay they in honor mean it. Teach them the conjugal happiness is not dependent on external decorum nor on the money of the husband, but simply and alone on his character. These things having been instilled, and they having understood them, then, if the time had arrived, have them marry without misgivings; they will find their way along unaided.

September 1994

Comment: *We include this item for comparison to today's approach to similar matters.*

FORMATION OF THE DODGE HISTORICAL SOCIETY

FORMATION OF THE DODGE HISTORICAL SOCIETY

Around 1991, a group of citizens began work to publish an updated history of Dodge County to be published by the local Daughters of the American Revolution society. The book they planned to publish followed upon Mrs. Wilton P. Cobb's *History of Dodge County*, which appeared in 1932.

The William Few Chapter of the DAR appointed Martha Saunders as Chairperson of the Committee. Serving with her were Betty Harrington and Mildred McCranie. Tom Harton, whose wife Margaret Burch Harton was Regent of the DAR, filled in for her after her untimely death. His work is a tribute to her interest and participation in many DAR projects through the years.

The Committee was assigned to produce a history covering the years 1932-1992, picking up where Mrs. Cobb's history left off. In 1993, the hard work of the Committee and many volunteers resulted in the publication of an 800-plus page book that was a worthy sequel to Mrs. Cobb's admirable history.

During this period the same group organized the Dodge Historical Society (first named the Dodge County Historical Society). Other founding members included Chester Saunders, William (Billy) Steele, Jean and Olin Pound, among many others.

In looking back to those times, three main objectives played a role in inspiring the creation of the Society. These were: (1) publication of the History in 1993; (2) determination to create and publish a record of all the cemeteries in Dodge County; and (3) the unexpected opportunity to purchase the Eastman House, then owned by Mrs. Sarah Bullock.

At first the Society met in the old Eastman Library on Fifth Avenue. Suitably, the Library building is located in what is known as Eastman Park. A monument to Mr. Eastman is located outside. The members requested funding from the City and the County and received generous assistance from them, which continues to the present. Fundraising also brought in funds from charter members interested in preserving the rich cultural heritage of our community.

A significant event occurred when Mrs. Sarah Bullock offered to sell the Eastman House to the Society. Mrs. Bullock's late husband Cary Bullock had inherited the Eastman House. His mother was a daughter of James

Bishop, who had purchased the house from the William Pitt Eastman family upon Mr. Eastman's death.

Purchase of the house by the Society was completed in October, 1993. Its renovation and preservation is an ongoing project carried out by Society members.

The last objective was the creation of a cemetery record and guide for finding ancestral grave sites. Martha and Chester Saunders, along with many other volunteers, worked for several years gathering material from local cemeteries. Tom Harton computerized the material and two published books were presented for sale.

At this time—2019—many of these founding members have passed on. They leave a legacy of a thriving Dodge Historical Society. The Eastman House continues to be improved and preserved. Public events are held at the house, along with the presentation of an impressive collection of historical artifacts.

All of Dodge County extends its appreciation to these founders and we strive to live up to the standard of hard work and dedication they invested in the Society.

The Board of Trustees of the Dodge Historical Society in 2019 consists of Phil Bearden, President and the Trustees are Connie Jones, Tom Peacock, Janice Purser, Rae Spradley and Gary Yawn.

When the Society was first organized, Lifetime memberships were established. The generosity of these early donors assisted in completing many projects associated with the Eastman House and other endeavors.

These Charter/Lifetime Members are listed below.

Eve Smith Allan
John A. and Priscilla Bennett
Cary G. Bullock
Irvin Bullock
Robert Bullock
Sarah I. Bullock
W. Dennis and Roxane Daniel
Donald and Barbara Dean
Doyle M. and Shirley B. Dillard
Lynda S. Franklin
Mr. and Mrs. E. M. Harrington, III
Col. Thomas G. Harton
Mr. and Mrs. Dan McCranie
Jimmy Pruett, Jr.
Martha and Chester Saunders
Hal. M. Smith, III
Mr. and Mrs. Hal M. Smith, Jr.
Maria Smith
Ray Smith
Dr. and Mrs. Wayne Smith
Col and Mrs. Will Ed Smith
Wayne C. Spear
W. Frank and Ann R. Stuckey
Dr. and Mrs. James Tison
James R. and LaMae Williams

THE DODGE HISTORICAL SOCIETY CEMETERY PROJECT

THE DODGE HISTORICAL SOCIETY CEMETERY PROJECT

A Short History

The recording of cemeteries is a fascinating project. The recorders became so engrossed in thinking of names, dates, and the variables found in every cemetery that the project becomes a pleasure rather than a chore. Much is written about the interesting epitaphs found in old cemeteries so it was expected that this would be the situation in Dodge County; however, Dodge County cemeteries are about a hundred years later than those with epitaphs. Nevertheless, many unique bits of information were found on individual graves. One woman had listed on her slab the names of three husbands with the length of each marriage. A man had three wives buried beside him and to be sure the public understood, a separate stone was at the foot of the graves with simply "first wife", "second wife" and so on.

There is a wide range of physical conditions found in cemeteries. The family type cemetery, when near the family home places is usually well kept, whereas the cemeteries where the families have moved away are fast deteriorating. Lack of care, unchecked growth of trees and brush, the free roaming of destructive animals and the unconscionable plowing over the graves by farmers and land clearing crews are the main reasons cemeteries disappear. The church cemeteries reflect the activity and interest within the church. An active church usually has a neat and well kept cemetery.

Besides the family and church cemeteries, there are community cemeteries, single grave sites and large city cemeteries. A cemetery on the Pulaski and Dodge boundary is divided by cemeteries next to each other and adjacent to the church but the identity of each is very carefully kept separate.

There are strict and clear federal laws protecting cemeteries and the law requires an accessible road and entrance to any burial plot.

The recording of the approximately 135 cemeteries in the county covered a period of five years plus the additional time the publishers worked on the completion of the book. Therefore, burials in the interim would not be recorded. It was noticed that many new pillow markers had been added in the last few years to the unmarked slabs. Unfortunately, if the particular cemetery with new markers had already been recorded, the names would not be on record. The recorders apologize if a loved one was left out for the above reasons and if in spite of care and concern a mistake was made by the recorders and caused an omission. Approximately 14,000 graves were recorded.

The customs of the times are found in cemeteries. For example, one particular tombstone we encountered gave the usual dates and information of the man and then it was engraved on his tombstone that he was murdered by two named men. This was stated and allowed to stay even though no trial had been held. In the world of today there would have been a lawsuit to have it removed.

In yesteryear a young girl was in disgrace if she had a baby out of wedlock. But today tiny infant graves can be found which have the mother and father of different names engraved on the infant's slab.

Advancements in science are realized when one sees multiple infant graves from earlier years lined up beside one mother. Ignorance in health and medicine, along with lack of access to medical services, brought on such sadness and unhappiness.

Of course the improvement of education is most noticeable. In the first cemetery which was recorded it was discovered that according to what was engraved a man died February 31. Incorrect spelling and unbelievable hyphenations were found throughout the county, especially when the graves were old.

Anger is so very evident when an eighteen year old wife is buried in her parents plot and it is engraved on her slab that she was killed by her husband.

Sadness is felt so strongly when especially children and young people are buried and their pictures are on the slab as well as toys suitable for them at that age.

Of course humor can be found everywhere, even in a cemetery. A middle-aged woman had an actual telephone sitting on her slab and you immediately know what she liked to do when she was living. And a man had a hog farm while living so he had a ceramic sow with six suckling piglets placed on his slab.

Pride is the word to describe the Orphans Cemetery which is located just outside Eastman. Each old plot is carefully fenced and the Williamson monument is so regal as it stands amidst the plots.

Patriotism is one of the strongest emotions felt throughout the cemeteries of the county. The U.S. government is gracious in furnishing for free a marker for any veteran on request. There are many, many markers and every single conflict by the United States is represented in the county as they are proudly placed by the grave of the veterans.

If one grave could be singled out by the recorders as the most impressive, it would have to be a fairly new one of a preacher. His name and appropriate dates were engraved at the top of the slab and at the bottom were three simple words, "Lord, I Tried." His influence still lives. Those who walk by his grave can only ask themselves, "Lord, have I really tried?"

A number of people over the years assisted in the work of copying these inscriptions and we deeply appreciate that. Hopefully, the following is complete but if there are omissions it was not intentional—Augusta B. Bennett, Marguerite W. Harden, Betty H. Harrington, Kay D. Miller, Carolyn Pridgen, and John D. Willcox. Col. Tom Harton was instrumental in typing up the information into a computerized database for publication.

Martha Saunders and Chester Saunders

UNMARKED GRAVES IN DODGE COUNTY

They are everywhere: on the tops of lonely hills, beside dusty roads, along quiet creek banks, and in the middle of plowed fields. They are the forgotten and abandoned graves of Dodge County citizens. Some of the graves, dating back to pioneer days, are older than the county.

When considering these burial places, the inevitable questions come to mind. Who are these people? Why were they buried where they are? Why were the graves abandoned? The history of one such grave is typical.

Herman Vewig brought his family to Dodge County sometime in the late 1800s. He came to act as the timber buyer for the Charles Godwin Lumber Company.

One winter morning, Mr. Vewig decided that the weather was right for killing hogs. Elsa, Mr. Vewig's four-year-old daughter, was fascinated by the bubbling pots of lard and moved too close to the fire. Before anyone noticed, she was enveloped in flames and badly burned. She died that afternoon.

In the first light of the next day, Mr. Vewig put the small coffin on his shoulder and walked to that part of his property bordering Sugar Creek. There he dug a grave and buried his youngest child. In 1908, Herman Vewig sold his property and moved his family to Atlanta. The grave was apparently never visited again by any member of the Vewig family.

The McCranie family is one of the original families of Dodge County. From this family have come State Senators, county officials, teachers and a host of outstanding citizens. Several pioneer members of this family were buried over a hundred years ago and rest today in unmarked graves in the middle of a large field in the Sand Grove Community.

In the fork of the old Eastman-Chauncey highway and the road to Parkerson Church are the unmarked graves of about 25 people. At one time a Methodist church stood nearby. Four or five of the people buried there were killed by logs falling from a sawmill log train. Mr. C. K. (Charlie) Brown was the only man who knew the names of these people. Now, Mr. Brown is gone, and their names are lost forever.

If one is persistent and is willing to fight the blackberry briars, haw bushes and honeysuckle vines, graves of many former black citizens can be found in an abandoned cemetery not far from the Harris Foster home. Such names as Lampkin, Shields, Northcutt, and Glover are there, and several government-issue headstones mark the graves of World War I veterans.

At Parkerson Church, along with the headstones to many members of the Hargrove Family, is a granite marker honoring Andrew Jackson Hargrove, one of Parkerson Church's earliest pastors. A casual visitor to the cemetery would assume that Brother Hargrove is buried there. He is not. Andrew Jackson Hargrove is buried in an abandoned cemetery on the Charles "Buddy" McCranie place, about three miles away.

Many of the county's early citizens rest in unmarked graves, but what they did with their lives is of more consequence than a name and date on a headstone. These are the men and women who carved a home out of a wilderness and created a county named Dodge.

As a Footnote: Martha and Chester Saunders, along with a group of volunteers, have recorded every cemetery in the County and it was a pleasant Sunday afternoon activity for about four years. The book of the 18,000 names was published in two volumes in the mid-1990s. The one disturbing thing which they encountered was the many graves which were unmarked. The average family and county church cemetery have about 25 percent unmarked graves which is unfortunate for those searching for ancestors. The related families are urged to add a headstone to those unmarked graves which they can still identify. Many cemeteries have disappeared for one reason or other and they are still being destroyed. Those who visit cemeteries will find humor, love, and history. It is well worth the time to do so.

Ovid Vickers, 1995

ACKNOWLEDGEMENTS

ACKNOWLEDGEMENTS

This project began with Mary Johnson Jowers, Eastman native. She became a member of the Dodge Historical Society in the early 1990s. The Dodge Historical Society acknowledges Ms. Jowers and thanks her for offering her papers for use in setting up a book of the material.

Board members Phil Bearden and Gary Yawn began the project by collating the records and arranging for local publishing company, MMJW BookHouse, to prepare a book. The company took on this project *gratis* with all income derived going to the Society. Additional Board members Connie Jones, Tom Peacock, Janice Purser and Rae Spradley are also acknowledged for their support.

Tonya Coleman completed the good work of typing up the manuscript. Josh Sheffield prepared the cover and interior design. Both are appreciated for their efforts and dedication in producing the work the readers now hold in their hands.

We also thank Judy Lowery and Coleman Gifts for serving as a vendor of the book. Ms. Lowery's dedication to providing an outlet for purchase of local history information offers a valuable public service to all of us.

It is fitting that in a book produced by a historical society that we look back to the founding members and extend our appreciation. Beginning in the early 1990s a group came together to form the Society. These included Betty Harrington, Tom Harton, Mildred McCranie, Chester Saunders and Martha Saunders as the core organizers. Others followed in promoting the Society. These citizens included Danny Pickett, Eleanor Pickett, Jean Pound, Olin Pound, William Steele, and many others.

In closing, let us extend our gratitude to those who prepared the newsletters and wrote the historical portions. These include Tad Evans, Stan McDaniel, Chester Saunders, Martha Saunders, Donnie Screws and Ovid Vickers, among others. Much of the history recounted in these stories exists for us only because these citizens took the time and energy to preserve their memories. Their efforts led to the production of this history collection for future citizens to learn from and enjoy.

SUGGESTED READINGS

SUGGESTED READINGS

Bartram, William. *Travels*. New York: Dover, 1955. Edited by Mark Van Doren.

Classic account of William Bartram's trek through the wilds of the southeastern United States from 1773-1778.

Chalker, Fussell M. *Pioneer Days Along the Ocmulgee*. Carrollton, Georgia: F. M. Chalker, 1970.

Unique and entertaining history of the Ocmulgee River, from its origins beneath the State Capitol building in Atlanta to its merging with the Oconee to form the mighty Altamaha River. Creek Indians, DeSoto, early settlers and more are featured.

Cobb, Mrs. Wilton P. *History of Dodge County*, 1932. Published in Washington: WPA Project Publication, 1932.

Mrs. Cobb prepared the History as a WPA Project during the Depression. She relied not only on written documents but on the reminiscences of older citizens who recalled the earliest days of Eastman and Dodge County.

Dodge Historical Society. *History of Dodge County, 1932-1992*. Eastman, Georgia: Dodge County Historical Society, 1993.

A sequel to Mrs. Cobb's 1932 *History*, this 800+ page book presents a panoramic view of the history of those sixty years. A great resource and an entertaining journey through later-day Dodge County's history.

Dodge, Phyllis B. *Tales of the Phelps-Dodge Family*. New York: New York Historical Society, 1987.

Family history of the Dodges, including William E. Dodge, his notable father, David Low Dodge, and others. The work offers detailed insight into William E. Dodge's business career.

Fishman, Gail. *Journeys through Paradise: Pioneering Naturalists in the Southeast*. Gainesville: University Press of Florida, 2000.

Engaging study of several intrepid explorers and naturalists as they traveled through the southeast.

Goff, John Hedges. *Placenames of Georgia: Essays of John H. Goff*. Edited by Frances Lee Utley and Marion Hemperley. Athens: University of Georgia Press, 1975, 2007.

Premier collection of Goff's essays on sites throughout Georgia. An essential Georgia history resource.

Hudson, Charles. *Knights of Spain, Warriors of the Sun.* Athens: University of Georgia Press, 1997.

Modern update on the route Spanish explorer DeSoto took through Georgia and the southeast in 1539-1542.

Lowitt, Richard. *A Merchant Prince of the Nineteenth Century: William E. Dodge.* New York: Columbia University Press, 1954.

Standard and well-researched biography of Dodge. In its 384 pages, the Dodge Land Wars rate less than two pages.

Lundberg, Patricia Yawn. *In the Piney Woods of Georgia: Pioneers in a Troubled Time.* Milledgeville, Georgia: Old Capital Press, 2007.

Pictures and text relate the Dodge Land Wars story along with material on the Yawn family of Dodge and Telfair counties.

Morrison, Carlton A. *Running the River: Poleboats, Steamboats & Timber Rafts on the Altamaha, Ocmulgee,*

Oconee and Ohoopee. St. Simons Island, Georgia: Saltmarsh Press, 2003.

Illustrated history of navigation in the Ocmulgee and Altamaha river basin.

Neel, Leon with Paul S. Sutter and Albert G. Way. *The Art of Managing Longleaf: A Personal History of the Stoddard-Neel Approach*. Athens: University of Georgia Press, 2010.

Scholarly and very readable account of one of the last wild areas of pine forest in Georgia.

Owsley, Frank. *Plain Folk of the Old South*. Baton Rouge: Louisiana State University Press, 1949.

Pioneering statistical study of ante-bellum farmers and planters with a contrarian economic view on slaveholding landowners.

Price, Eugenia. *St. Simons Memoir*. New York: J. B. Lippincott, 1977.

Accessible and informative recounting of Ms. Price's discovery of St. Simons Island and her subsequent historical novels based on its early inhabitants, including the Dodge family.

Snow, Frankie. *An Archaeological Survey of the Ocmulgee Big Bend Region*. Douglas, Georgia: South Georgia College, 1977.

Pioneering scholarly study of the area's original inhabitants and their geographical distribution throughout the area.

Steele, William J. "Railroads of Dodge County." Excerpt contained in the *History of Dodge County, 1932-1992*. Eastman, GA: William Few Chapter, DAR, 1993.

Excellent essay on the railroads and tram roads of early Dodge, Telfair and adjacent counties.

Talley, J. N. *The Dodge Lands and Litigation*. Atlanta: Annual Report of the Georgia Bar Association, 1925.

Address given by Talley summing up the Dodge Land Wars. Mr. Talley was the legal referee concluding more than fifty years of legal wrangling in the case.

Tripp, Mary Ellen. *Longleaf Pine Lumber Manufacturing in the Altamaha River Basin, 1865-1918*. Ann Arbor: University Microfilms International, 1983.

Ms. Tripp's (now Wilson) doctoral thesis on the timber industry in the Ocmulgee area provides insight and background to the Dodge Land issues.

Walker, Jane and Trowell, Chris. *The Dodge Land Troubles: 1868-1923*. Fernandina Beach, Florida: Wolfe Publishing, 2004.

The massive undertaking by the authors addresses not only the Land Troubles but also the history of the Ocmulgee area. With facsimiles of newspaper articles and original essays on the topic, this essential resource covers the period 1800 to 1923.

Wetherington, Mark V. *The New South Comes to Wiregrass Georgia*. Knoxville: University of Tennessee Press, 1994.

Mr. Wetherington's pioneering study of the wiregrass area of South Georgia and the socioeconomic changes occurring from 1860-1910 augments the history of the Dodge County. A good study of the area and formation of Eastman and Dodge County is included in the book.

Whigham, Stephen (Editor). *The Lightwood Chronicles: Being the True Story of Brainard Cheney's novel, Lightwood*. Eastman, Georgia: MM John Welda BookHouse, 2012.

A collection of historical material related to the Dodge Land Wars and the timber companies.

INDEX

Index

Armstrong, Major Charles R.
   Postmaster 173
Arthur, Mrs. James M.
   (Mary Helen Willcox) . 27
Ashburn, W. W.................10
Basketball, Girl's 163
Bearden, Phil.................181
Bishop, Estelle................. 45
Bishop, James, Jr............ 44
Bishop, James, Sr....... 11, 43
Bishop, Simeon 43
Bland, T. A. 96
Bracewell, Justin............144
Bracewell, Mary Jean.....145
Brown, Jordan................. 67
Buchan, Dr. James Monroe
   ....6, 51
Buchan, Mattie.................51
Bullock, Cary 32, 180
Bullock, Sarah 180
Burns, Orene Mullis........ 76
Calhoun, B. R.
   Attorney........................ 79
Campbell, Helena Eastman
   Ogden 25, 31
Carlyle, Thomas i
Carroll, T. K. 93

Chauncey, Georgia 99
Chauncey, William 4
Chester Banking Company
  85
Chester, Georgia.............. 83
Chicken Road
   aka Chickasaw Path 83
Clark, Matthew 10
Clements, Walter M.
   Attorney........................ 79
Cobb, Mrs. Wilton P.. ii, 179
Coffee, Grady 5
Coffee, L. M. (Family) ... 150
Cofield, Audrey Hargrove 67
Coleman Hardware 130
Copeland, Georgia........... 90
Court House (1872) 6
Currie, John T. 85
Daniel, Nancy J. 43
De Lietch (Hotel)
   Photograph................ 122
Deese, Alto 97
Deese, Edith Bland.......... 97
DeLacy, John F........9, 11, 78
Dennis, Gene and Mimi ..58
Dodge County Court House
  75
Dodge Park 62

Dodge, A. G. P. 11
Dodge, George E. 48
Dodge, William E. ... 4, 7, 46
  Court House donation 46
  Statue in New York City
    115
Eastman Academy 40
Eastman Bakery 137
Eastman Bus Station 73
Eastman Hotel Company 11, 69
Eastman House 55, 58
  Sold to Dodge Historical
    Society 180
Eastman Post Office 157
  WPA Mural 157
Eastman, Arthur 3
Eastman, Caro 4
  Marriage 14
Eastman, Deborah Greeley
    .... 1, 12
Eastman, Ebenezer 1, 2
Eastman, Helena Dekay
    Fondey 4, 13
Eastman, Roger 1
Eastman, Samuel Jr. 1
Eastman, Samuel, Sr. 1
Eastman, William Pitt 2, 7, 10
  Burial in Woodlawn
    Cemetery 27
  Death 15
  Land Holdings 10
  Last Will and Testament
    23
  Letter with biographical
    information 35
  Obituary 16, 18
  Portrait of 26, 114
  Resolution 20
Edwards, T. H. 137

Edwards. W. C. 62
Evans, Tad 1, 196
Fondey, Isaac 4
Foster, General Ira 8, 44
Garrett, Bertie Mae 146
Georgia Land and Lumber
  Company 4, 38
Gilmanton, New
  Hampshire 1, 36
Godwinsville Community
    162
Gregory, Irene 133
Guyton, Mary E. 43
Guyton, Moses 43
Hall, Luther A. 9
Ham, H. W. J.
  Newspaper Editor 172
Hargrove Crossing 66
Hargrove, Andrew Jackson
    .... 66, 191
Hargrove, Jane 67
Hargrove, Larkin 66
Hargrove, Nancy Hendley
    66
  Photograph 118
Harrington, Betty 179
Harrington, Wilton D.
  Attorney 79
Harton, Margaret Burch 179
Harton, Tom 147, 179
Hazlehurst, George H. 5
Herrman, Elias
  Attorney 79
*History of Dodge County
  (1932)* ii
*History of Dodge County,
  1932-1992* iii
Hosford, E. C.
  Architect for Courthouse
    75
Jackson, R. L. 85

Jarrard, Jason (Family)..150
Jaybird Springs 95
Jessup, W. B. 84
Johns, Aurelia 137
Johns, Ralph 137
Jones, Connie 181
Jowers, Mary Johnson..... ii, 195
Kansas City Special (Train) 140
Lee Land Hotel................ 72
  Photograph................123
Lee, William (Billy)............ 5
Lewis, R. C.
  House 62
Log House (Single Pen and Double Pen) 66
Long, Paul
  Basketball Coach........163
Macon and Brunswick Railroad.................. 3, 47
Malone's Lake 87
Maloy, Dr. W. C................ 92
McCranie Family........... 190
McCranie, Edward L. (Family).....................150
McCranie, Mildred.........179
McCranie, W. D.
  County Commissioner 76
McDaniel, Dr. Tom (Family).....................150
McDaniel, Stan
  Postmaster 157
McMillan, T. A. 95, 96
Milner, B. S.
  Attorney....................... 79
Minstrel Shows 169
Montgomery, Idolene Fitzgerald 70
Mullin, James.................. 99
Mullingar

section of Chauncey, Georgia 99
Myrick, Nellie Harrell ... 149
Myrick, Victor................ 149
Ogden, Caro Eastman
  Daughter...................... 14
Ogden, Helena Eastman . 14
Ogden, James Monroe.... 14
Ogden, Susan Eastman ... 14
Orphans Cemetery
  Williamson monument 50
Pate, Anthony C. (Judge) 78
Peacock, Tom..................181
Phelps, Melissa................46
Place names in Dodge County........................ 107
Pound, Jean 180
Pound, Olin.................... 180
Presbyterian Church (Eastman)...................... 9
Purser, Janice 181
Quilting in Dodge County 160
Reid, Emory...................... 76
Rhine, Georgia.................90
Rogers, Doug 88
Rogers, James Cullen (J.C.)
  Sheriff 62
Saunders, Cece 150
Saunders, Chester 152, 181, 192
Saunders, Chester (Family) 150
Saunders, Martha 146, 152, 179, 192
Screws, Donnie................89
Sheffield, Josh 210
Sheldon, J. W...................... 9
Sheldon, Martha............. 130
Smith, D. D. 30

Smith, D. D. (Family).... 150
Smith, E. A.
    Attorney....................... 79
Smith, Julia 152
    Attorney....................... 79
Smith, Will Ed
    Attorney....................... 79
Spradley, Rae...................181
Station No. 13 5
Studstill, Lee....................137
Swymer, James M. 90
Telephone in Chauncey... 99
Uplands Hotel 12, 68
    Photograph 120
Vewig, Herman.............. 190
Vickers, Ovid 153, 196
    Poems 141

Walker, Carrie..................96
Weaver, D. W...................10
Whigham, John (Family)
   150
Wilbanks, Annie 129
Wilbanks, John T.............73
Willcox, John D. 1, 27
William Few Chapter, DAR
    179
Williamson, A. G..............50
    Mausoleum in Orphans Church Cemetery... 116
Woodlawn Cemetery
    Association......................9
Wooten, J. E.
    Attorney 79
Yawn, Gary..................... 181

Printed on Acid Free Paper.

Cover and Interior Design provided by Josh Sheffield

For additional information on Dodge County, Georgia and related publications, please contact the publisher at the address indicated in the front matter of this work.

www.ingramcontent.com/pod-product-compliance
Lightning Source LLC
Chambersburg PA
CBHW030854170426
43193CB00009BA/609